—THE—
EDINA RONAY KNITWEAR COLLECTION

ST. MARTIN'S PRESS
NEW YORK

ISBN 0-312-02384-7

Library of Congress Catalog Card Number: 88-043057

First published in Great Britain by Sidgwick & Jackson Limited
under the title *The Edina Ronay Collection*.

First U.S. Edition

10 9 8 7 6 5 4 3 2 1

ACKNOWLEDGEMENTS

This book would never have been more than a nice
idea without the unbelievable help and support from:
Caroline Baker who styled the fashion, looked after
the models and in general made all our lives so
much happier while shooting the pictures;
Hans Feurer who, against all odds, came up with
the great photographs in this book;
Dick Polak who took the still life pictures
and after all these years is still with me;
Martin Morris who did the hair and helped
with so many other things;
Frances Hathaway who created such natural make-up;
Lene Hyltoft, Lindsey Thurlow, Bill, Paul, Alaric,
Laura, Aaliya, Max, Shebah and Lula our dog
who modelled the knitwear so beautifully;
Ray Gautier and Hilary Krag who have put
so much into making this book look great;
Joan Latham, Sue Turton and especially Sharon Peake
without whom I could not have finished this project;
Stephen Sheard who dyed the yarns to my specifications;
Tony Brook for all his patience;
Penny Massot and all our wonderful and
loyal staff at the studio;
Janet Bentley who checked all the patterns;
Sarah Campion, Gill Paul and Robert Smith and,
of course, all those skilful knitters around Britain who
have helped us so much over the years.

CONTENTS

Fashion for me, is not just about clothes and the mood of the season. It's about originality, style, quality, craftsmanship, tradition and heritage. I have always especially loved the work of traditional craftsmen and women; fine hand-made lace, ethnic embroideries, handpainted ceramics and, of course, handknits.

In the 1960's, I had a small shop selling antique lace and clothes, specialising in the styles of the 30's and 40's. I have always been very interested in the sweaters of these periods. They represented something very attractive to me, with their complex stitch details and fantastic Fair Isle patterns.

I used to look around in jumble sales, street markets and auction rooms to find these old sweaters. I would select the parts and stitches I liked best and use them, re-coloured, in my new and contemporary shaped designs. At that time there was a dwindling group of traditional handknitters in Britain. I asked some of them to make up my designs and hoped that while selling my sweaters alongside the antique clothes in my shop, my efforts could also help to keep this creative craft alive. Little did I expect then that my ideas would take off in the way they did.

The next stage came when a friend in the fashion business suggested that other shops might want to sell my sweaters as well, so I made up a small collection and took it to an international buyers' fair in London. The sweaters were an immediate success, I couldn't believe it! We were inundated with orders from America as well as Britain, and invited to sell the collection at fashion fairs in Paris and New York where the orders continued and increased. That was ten years ago and my business has grown and grown ever since.

Five years after that first collection, we decided that we should extend our traditional range to include

Edina Ronay at work, looking over some new designs. Right: close-up of an antique kelim.

some younger and bolder designs. This is the part of the collection which American fashion buyers call 'directional' as opposed to the 'classical' sweaters. I enjoy working with modern, abstract patterns but I often find that the newest, most contemporary designs have their origins in traditional and ethnic sources.

For the last fifteen years I have been collecting beautiful and inspiring objects that catch my eye; baskets with an unusual weave, handpainted plates and jugs in wonderful colours, ornaments from the 30's and 40's, antique boxes from India made of papier-mâché and, of course, many beautiful old books, as well as embroidered clothes, lace table-cloths, shawls, old photo frames and 1940's costume jewellery.

Most of this collection consists of inexpensive objects, bought because they are beautiful and decorative never for their value in monetary terms. Recently, I have also been buying more expensive antiques; embroidered cushions, ornate mirrors, mother-of-pearl and flowered Victorian boxes, and kelims. The modern ones still have wonderful colours but my favourites are the really old ones in which the colours have faded to beautiful, muted shades.

I also love the colours and fine brushwork of the old Indian Moghul paintings at the Victoria and Albert Museum in London. Raoul Dufy is a great favourite of mine. A few years ago there was an exhibition at the Hayward Gallery in London of Dufy's paintings and some fantastic designs he did for Poiret's fabrics. Sometimes I find my inspiration at these exhibitions. For example, when I went to see the 'Oh India' exhibition at the Metropolitan Museum in New York,

Antique papier-mâché boxes from Kashmir and one of my favourite hand-painted jugs.

I was so impressed by the stunning embroideries of animals worked in brilliant, vibrant colours on silk, that the following season I included some 'animal' sweaters in bright primary colours in my collection.

Traditional and tribal costumes from around the world are another source of inspiration: the dazzling splendour of Russian Imperialist costumes, the vivid colours of African tribal costumes and jewellery, the heavy decoration of Korean wedding costumes and antique Chinese pleated skirts. When I travel I always look at the detail in authentic local garments. In Morocco, I was fascinated by the way the women put together marvellous outfits by just wrapping brightly coloured cloths around themselves. Accessorised with

lots of silver and amber jewellery they look really fantastic. I am particularly fond of a very fine wool cape I bought out there in a local suk.

On my travels, I also look out for shops selling books on the local crafts, such as appliqué, beading and embroidery. These books often provide inspiration for a new design, but the most important influence on my work is the wonderfully rich tradition of my native Hungary.

After I was last there, on holiday, I came home with piles of colourful antique garments, bits of embroidery and books on the local skills. The gypsy and peasant women of old Hungary used to make elaborate beaded, pleated, sequinned and embroi-

Detail of a Chinese print.

dered clothes as a dowry for their daughters. They were kept in trunks and only bought out for special occasions like weddings, saint's days and festivals. If times were hard they could be sold, but otherwise they were passed on through the generations. The beauty of design and use of flowered patterns everywhere will inspire me for a long time to come.

My parents lived in Budapest before the Second World War. At that time it was equalled only by Paris as an artistic and cultural centre in Europe. Our family owned several restaurants, the most famous of which was the Belvarosi, an elegant, galleried restaurant in the heart of the city where all the writers, actors, musicians, film-makers and local politicians would gather to talk, drink, eat and, most importantly, to be seen. My parents and grandparents were very much a part of this life. Every evening my grandmother, who was a great social lady, would have her hair styled and dress up in couture clothes and beautiful jewellery to go to the restaurant to hold court.

The family lost everything during the war. Immediately afterwards, my father was far-sighted enough to realise the political situation was changing and that things were going to be very different in the future. He had studied law at Cambridge and still had a few English connections from that time, so they packed up and moved to England to start a new life. He owned a restaurant in London before he started the Egon Ronay Guide, which was an immediate success. Over the years, he has been quite instrumental in changing the style and quality of restaurant food in Britain.

My mother has always been very chic and beautiful. She dresses with great style. In Hungary, I remember her wardrobe was full of handstitched suits and dresses and custom-made hats and shoes. My father, too, is very stylish. When my parents came to England, their financial circumstances changed dramatically, but they continued to care very much about their appearance. My mother and her friends, members of the exiled Hungarian community, would always dress up for tea, dinner parties and even just at home. So an interest in quality and style was instilled in me from an early age and it was this interest which has been so important in my career.

As a child, I loved to paint and draw and I was happiest with a paintbrush and a sheet of paper. My father encouraged my interest in art and he allowed me to leave school at the age of sixteen to study fashion at St Martin's School of Art in London. However, after only one year at St Martin's, I was spotted by a film producer and cast in my first movie.

Detail of a beaded Hungarian apron.
Right: close-up of a woven Central African basket.

Later I worked in repertory theatre and went to RADA to study acting. London in the late 60's was a very exciting place to be. The film industry was booming and I met many famous actors, directors, writers and musicians. My husband, Dick Polak, was a film producer when I met him. He gave me the leading role in the film he was making and we've been together ever since.

After making that film and directing me in another, we spent a year travelling – living in Morocco, Ibiza and Formentera. When we returned to London we found a declining film industry and I decided to work as a model. It was while modelling that I started collecting and selling antique lace and clothes; I had finally returned to my true love, fashion.

Designing sweaters will always be very attractive to me, but gradually I have found myself drawn into other areas. I began to design trousers and skirts, originally just to complement the sweaters in our shop. They sold so well that we decided to put together a proper wholesale collection for the New York, Paris, Milan and London shows. My designs are now sold all over the world – in America, Australia, Canada, Japan, and Europe.

Our clients include some of the most elegant and beautiful women in the world. Selina Scott and the Duchess of York are regular customers and the Princess of Wales, the Duchess of Kent, Patricia Hodge and Elaine Page also wear my clothes. Lauren Bacall, Jacqueline Bisset and Charlotte Rampling among others visit my shop whenever they're in town.

I hope that through the patterns in this book we will reach many more people and give them the same pleasure out of wearing the sweaters as I get out of designing them. Handknitting is very special. It's creative, it's fun and it is always in fashion.

KNITTING NOTES

MEASUREMENTS

Measurements are given in both metric and imperial. You can work in whichever you prefer as long as you follow the same system throughout the pattern. Before you start, check the measurements given for each garment and adjust them as necessary. Most of the garments are designed to fit loosely, as can be seen if you compare the 'to fit' measurements with the 'actual measurements'.

Figures in brackets refer to the larger sizes. Where only one figure is given this refers to all sizes.

TENSION

To achieve a garment measuring the same as the instructions, your tension *must* be correct. Please take time to check this before you start knitting your garment. Check your tension on a test square, and if you have fewer stitches than the given tension, use needles a size smaller than those recommended in the pattern; if you have more stitches than the given tension, then use needles a size larger. Keep changing your needle sizes until you have the correct size for the tension being worked.

Please note that these are designer patterns and as such the needle sizes and tension may be different from that recommended by the spinner on the ball band.

YARN

These garments have been knitted in specified yarns to achieve the result illustrated, but any yarns can be used if they are the correct weight and knit to the given tension.

Please note that the amounts of yarn specified are based on average requirements and the amounts given are therefore only approximate. They are measured in grammes. For the American knitter, 1 ounce = approximately 28.35 grammes.

CHARTS

When reading charts, work K rows (odd numbered rows) from right to left and P rows (even numbered rows) from left to right, unless instructed otherwise in a particular design. Each square of the chart refers to one stitch and one row.

COLOUR KNITTING

Stranding and Block knitting are two methods of working coloured knitting and motifs which should be used when working designs from this book. When working either method a close check must be kept on tension. Before starting, it is a good idea to wind off small amounts of the coloured yarns required onto stiff pieces of card called bobbins. This makes working in different colours much easier as you are not handling large balls of yarn which will become twisted and knotted.

STRANDING. This is most useful where there are small areas between colours, and where not more than two colours are used on one row. For this method the yarn is carried across the back of the work, when not in use, from one position to the next, usually not over more than 3 stitches at a time, unless otherwise instructed. The stranding must be kept even, otherwise the garment will stretch or pucker.

BLOCK KNITTING. When working large areas of one colour, use separate balls of yarn for each area, winding yarn onto bobbins. At each colour change, yarn from each bobbin or ball must be twisted with the colour next to it otherwise a small hole will result. When the last stitch of one colour has been worked, lay the yarn to the left and bring the next colour to be worked up and around it in place. On the next row the colour will be passed the opposite way thus making a ladder appearance on the wrong side.

AMERICAN KNITTERS

Both metric and imperial measurements are used throughout the book. American needle sizes are also given, so the patterns should be easily followed by American knitters. However, there are a few differences in knitting terminology and yarn names which are given below:

UK	US
cast off	bind off
stocking stitch	stockinette stitch
tension	gauge
work straight	work even
Aran	fisherman/ medium weight
double knitting	knitting worsted
4-ply	lightweight

CIRCULAR NEEDLES

A number of patterns in this book use a circular needle for the collar or neckband. Many knitters refuse to try these needles, but they are in fact very easy to use. Circular needles are made of flexible plastic with knitting needles at both ends and can be bought in different lengths, depending on the job they are intended for. Do not buy one too long for the job intended as it will stretch the work out of shape; aim to buy one that will enable the stitches to reach the needle points at both ends without stretching the knitting.

PRESSING

Follow the instructions given with the yarn, usually on the ball band label. Do not press the ribbing. Each piece of the garment should be pressed separately to the measurements given in the pattern. Place each piece on the ironing board with the wrong side uppermost and use a damp (or dry, or wet) cloth according to yarn label instructions. Press by raising and lowering the iron, do not move it about as in ordinary ironing. If you are using several qualities of yarn, use the coolest setting suggested. If pressing is not recommended for one of the yarns then do not press at all.

SEWING UP

Invisible seams should be used for the side and sleeve seams, where the seam runs in the direction of the knitting. Back stitched seams should be used where the seam runs across the direction of the knitting, as in the shoulder seams.

When more than one colour yarn has been used, finish the ends off by using a blunt-ended wool needle and darn the ends in along the colour join on the wrong side.

SHOULDER PADS

The appearance of garments with set in sleeves is greatly enhanced by the addition of shoulder pads. Some of the designs in this book have shoulder pads, but you can in fact add them to any design which you think would benefit from them.

Shoulder pad knitting instructions are given under the appropriate patterns but the following instructions should be noted when sewing them in position.

Fold cast-on edge of shoulder pad in half to find centre line. Place this line along shoulder seam on wrong side of work, ensuring that the cast-on edge of pad is protruding slightly into puff sleeve. Pin into place, ensuring pad is not pulling at any point. Sew loosely into place at the three corners only.

For a more padded effect, two sections can be knitted, stuffed lightly with wadding or thin foam and then all three edges closed.

ABBREVIATIONS

Special abbreviations relating only to one particular design are given under the instructions for that pattern.

A to J = contrast colours
alt = alternate(ly)
approx = approximately
beg = begin(ning)
cm = centimetre(s)
CN = cable needle
cont = continu(e)(ing)
dec = decreas(e)(ing)
D.K. = double knitting
foll = follow(s)(ing)
g = gram(s)
g st = garter stitch
in = inch(es)
inc = increas(e)(ing)
K = knit
K1B = K 1 below, knit into next stitch one row below, at the same time slipping off stitch above
MC = main colour
mm = millimetres
P = purl
patt = pattern
psso = pass slipped stitch over
rem = remain(s)(ing)
rep = repeat(s)
rs = right side of work
sl = slip
st(s) = stitch(es)
st st = stocking stitch
tbl = through back of loop
tog = together
ws = wrong side of work
yb = yarn back
yf = yarn forward
yon = yarn over needle
yrn = yarn round needle

AFRICAN FAIR ISLE

The idea behind this sweater was to use a basic Fair Isle pattern but enlarged many times. The colours were inspired by a book about African tribes. I love the bright primary colours the tribespeople used for painting their faces and the vivid purples, reds and yellows of their huge necklaces and bangles. The short, cropped shape of this sweater gives it a youthful, casual look and it can be worn at any time of year with blue jeans, ethnic skirts or ski pants. Lauren Bacall bought one when it first came out.

MEASUREMENTS

One size only to fit bust
86–102cm (34–40in).
Actual measurement
126cm (49½in).
Full length 58cm (23in).
Sleeve seam 40cm (15¾in).

MATERIALS

Rowan Handknit D.K. Cotton
50g balls.
Main colour (MC) turkish plum
(277) 11 balls;
1st contrast colour (A) old
amethyst (278) 5 balls;
2nd contrast colour (B) clover
(266) 3 balls;
3rd contrast colour (C) cherry
(298) 4 balls;
4th contrast colour (D) fuchsia
(272) 2 balls;
5th contrast colour (E) yellow
(271) 2 balls.
Equivalent yarn: D.K.
1 pair each of 3¾mm (US 4) and
4mm (US 5) knitting needles.
One 3¾mm (US 4) short circular
needle.
2 spare needles.

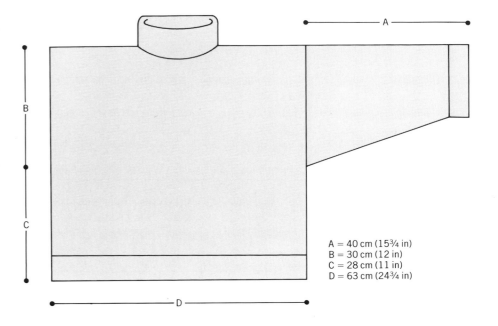

A = 40 cm (15¾ in)
B = 30 cm (12 in)
C = 28 cm (11 in)
D = 63 cm (24¾ in)

TENSION

20 sts and 28 rows to 10cm (4in)
on 4mm (US 5) needles over st st.
See page 10.

BACK

With 3¾mm (US 4) needles and
MC, cast on 130 sts and work in
double rib as foll:
1st row (rs facing) K2, *P2, K2,
rep from * to end.
2nd row P2, *K2, P2, rep from *
to end.
Rep last 2 rows for 6cm (2½in),

ending with a 2nd row.
Change to 4mm (US 5) needles
and starting with a K row work in
st st from chart, rep the 26 st patt
5 times across row.
Cont straight foll chart until
122nd row has been worked.
Now cont in MC only and work
8 rows in st st.
Shape back neck
Next row (rs facing) K48 sts,
turn, K2 tog, P to end and work
on this last set of 47 sts only.
**Dec 1 st at neck edge on every
row until 43 sts rem.
Cast off.
Return to rem sts and place centre
34 sts on a spare needle, with rs
facing rejoin yarn to rem sts and
K to end of row.
Now work as for first side from **
to end.

FRONT

Work as for back until 114 rows
of chart have been worked.
Shape front neck
Next row (rs facing) Patt 48,
turn, K2 tog, patt to end and work
on this last set of 47 sts only.
***Keeping patt correct, and
when chart is complete cont in
MC only, as for back, dec 1 st at
neck edge on every row until 43

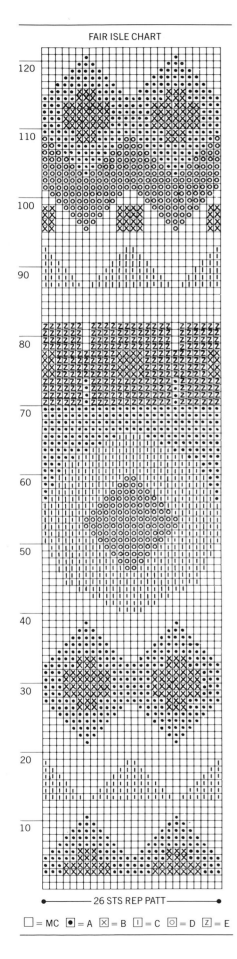

FAIR ISLE CHART

— 26 STS REP PATT —

☐ = MC   ● = A   ⊠ = B   Ⅰ = C   ⊙ = D   ℤ = E

sts rem. Now cont straight until front measures same as back to cast-off shoulder edge, ending on same patt row.
Cast off.
Return to rem sts and place centre 34 sts on a spare needle, with rs facing rejoin yarn to rem sts and patt to end of row.
Now work as for first side from *** to end.

SLEEVES

With 3¾mm (US 4) needles and MC, cast on 78 sts and work in double rib as for back welt for 5cm (2in), ending with a 2nd row. Change to 4mm (US 5) needles and starting with a K row work in st st from chart, rep the 26 st patt 3 times across row, *at the same time*, inc 1 st at both ends of every foll 3rd row until there are 126 sts on the needle, working inc sts into the patt.
Now cont straight until 86th row of chart has been worked, thus

ending with a ws row.
Cast off fairly loosely using MC.
Rep patt for second sleeve.

ROLL COLLAR

Join both shoulder seams.
With the 3¾mm (US 4) circular needle and MC and rs facing, pick up and K 19 sts down left front neck, K the 34 sts at centre front, pick up and K 19 sts up right front neck, 5 sts down right back neck, K the 34 sts at centre back and finally pick up and K 5 sts up left back neck. (116 sts)
Work in rounds of K2, P2, rib for 30cm (12in).
Cast off loosely ribwise.

TO MAKE UP

With centre of cast-off edges of sleeves to shoulder seams, sew sleeves carefully in position reaching down to same patt row on front and back. Join side and sleeve seams matching patt. Roll collar onto right side.

WILLOW-PATTERN SWEATER

Most willow-patterned china is based on the old Japanese myth of the two lovers who cannot get married so they run away together and turn into doves. You can see the lovers crossing a bridge on this sweater. The perfect summer cover-up, it is very loose and comfortable to wear and looks wonderful with navy blue spotted fabrics, cream or plain navy. One of the royal princesses bought this sweater.

MEASUREMENTS

To fit bust 86–97(102–112)cm
(34–38(40–44)in).
Actual measurement 120(136)cm
(47¼(53½)in).
Full length 68cm (26¾in).
Sleeve seam 39cm (15½in).

MATERIALS

Rowan Handknit D.K. Cotton
50g balls.
Main colour (MC) ecru (251)
14(15) balls;
Contrast colour (C) turkish plum
(277) 5(5) balls.
Equivalent yarn: D.K.
1 pair each of 3¾mm (US 4) and
4mm (US 5) knitting needles.
One 3¼mm (US 4) short circular
needle.

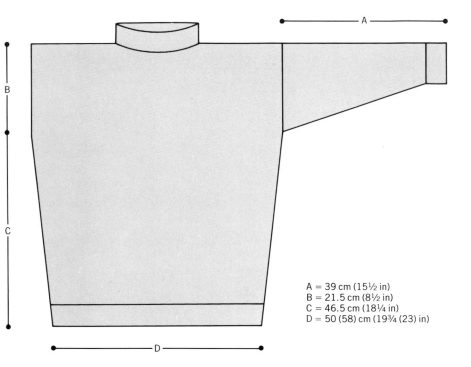

A = 39 cm (15½ in)
B = 21.5 cm (8½ in)
C = 46.5 cm (18¼ in)
D = 50 (58) cm (19¾ (23) in)

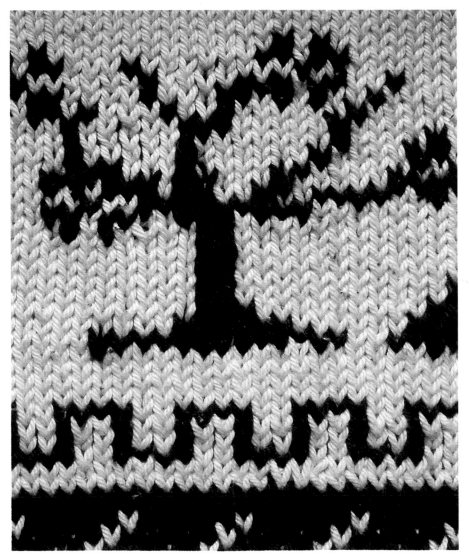

TENSION

20 sts and 28 rows to 10cm (4in)
on 4mm (US 5) needles over st st.
See page 10.

BACK

With 3¾mm (US 4) needles and
MC cast on 100(116) sts and work
in two-tone double rib as foll,
carrying yarn not in use loosely
across ws:
1st row (rs facing) *K2C, P2MC,
rep from * to end.
2nd row *K2MC, P2C, rep from
* to end.
Rep these 2 rows until rib
measures 5cm (2in), ending with
a 2nd row.
Change to 4mm (US 5) needles
and starting with a K row work in
st st from chart, working between
appropriate lines for size required,
at the same time, inc 1 st at both
ends of 11th row and then every
foll 12th row as indicated until
there are 120(136) sts on the
needle.
Now cont straight until 166th row
has been worked, thus ending
with a ws row.
Shape back neck
Next row Patt 47(55), turn, work

BACK AND FRONT CHART

NECK SHAPING

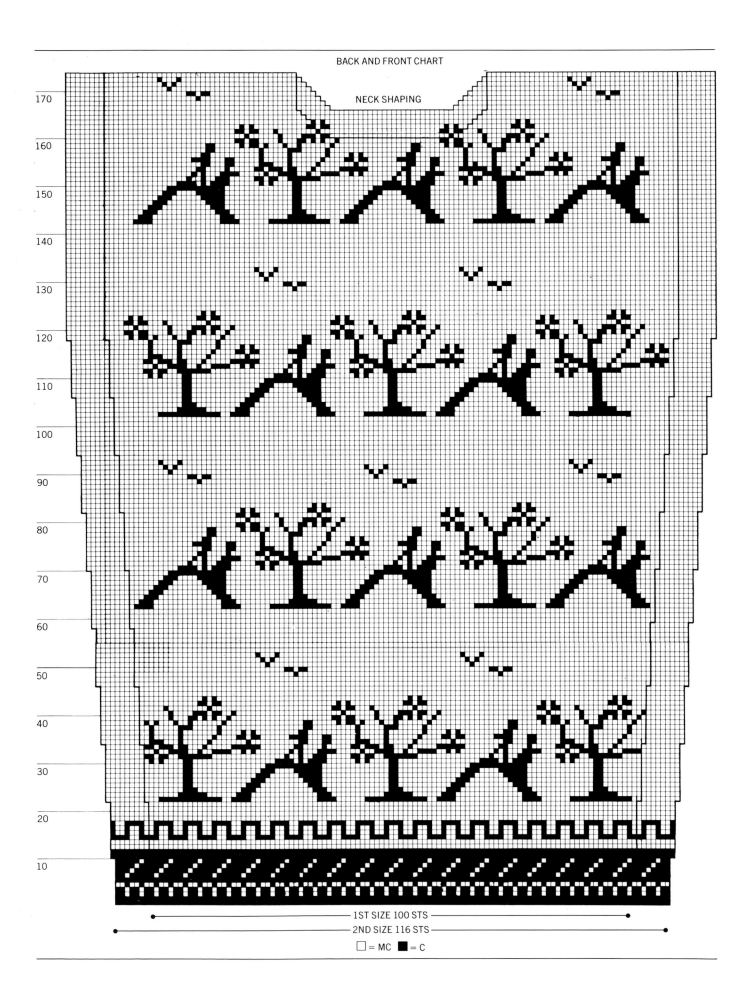

1ST SIZE 100 STS
2ND SIZE 116 STS

□ = MC ■ = C

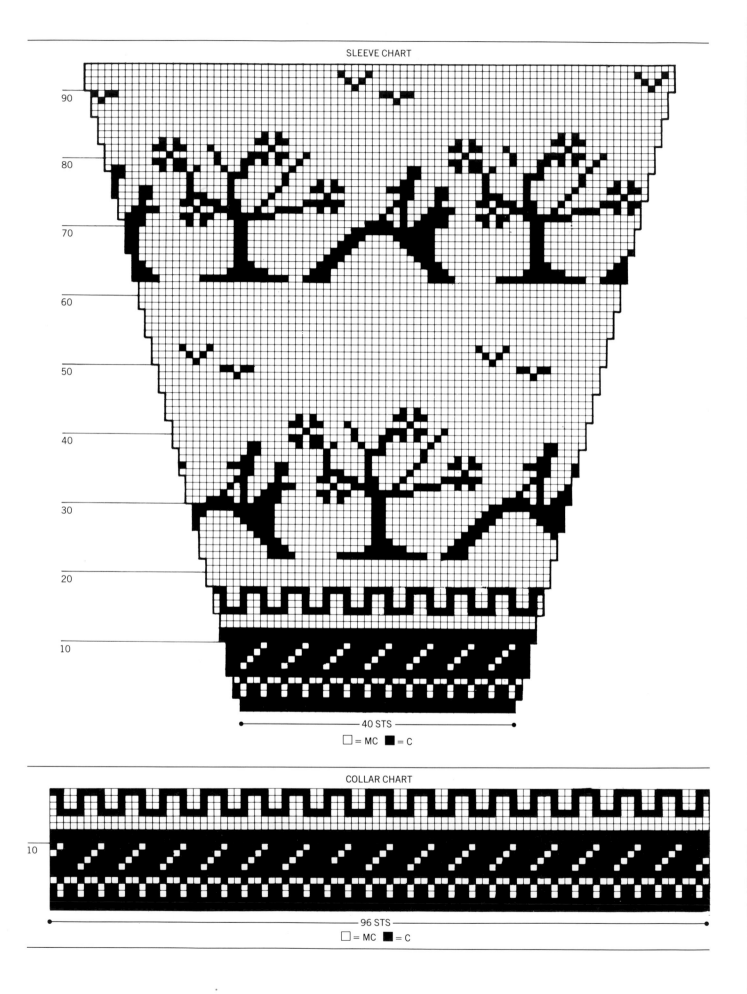

SLEEVE CHART

90
80
70
60
50
40
30
20
10

40 STS

☐ = MC ■ = C

COLLAR CHART

10

96 STS

☐ = MC ■ = C

2 tog and patt to end of row and work on this last set of 46(54) sts only.

**Keeping patt correct dec 1 st at neck edge on every row until 40(48) sts rem. Cast off.

With rs facing rejoin yarn to rem sts, cast off centre 26 sts and patt to end of row.

Next row Patt to last 2 sts, work 2 tog.

Now work as for first side from ** to end.

FRONT

Work as for back until 160th row has been worked, thus ending with a ws row.

Shape front neck

Next row Patt 46(54), turn, work 2 tog and patt to end of row and work on this last set of 45(53) sts only.

***Keeping patt correct dec 1 st at neck edge on every row until 40(48) sts rem. Now work straight until front measures same as back to cast-off shoulder edge. Cast off. With rs facing rejoin yarn to rem sts, cast off centre 28 sts and patt to end of row.

Next row Patt to last 2 sts, work 2 tog.

Now work as for first side from *** to end.

SLEEVES

With 3¾mm (US 4) needles and MC cast on 40 sts and work in two-tone double rib as for back welt for 5cm (2in), ending with a 2nd row.

Change to 4mm (US 5) needles and starting with a K row work in st st foll sleeve chart, shaping as indicated at both ends of 3rd row and then every foll 4th row, working inc sts into patt as shown. When 86 sts are on the needle cont straight until chart is complete.

Cast off fairly loosely.

Rep patt for second sleeve.

COLLAR

Join both shoulder seams.

With the 3¾mm (US 4) circular needle and rs facing and MC, pick up and K 42 sts from around back neck and 54 sts from around front neck. (96 sts)

Now starting with a K round, work in rounds of st st (every round K) working from row 4 to 18 on chart as indicated.

Now work a further 14 rounds in st st in MC.

Cast off fairly loosely.

TO MAKE UP

With centre of cast-off edges of sleeves to shoulder seams sew sleeves carefully in position reaching down to same depth on front and back. Join side and sleeve seams. Fold collar in half to inside and sl st loosely in position. To keep welts in shape, shirring elastic can be added to ribbings at lower edges.

SWEATER WITH CUPPED CABLES

T his is a classic shape for a child's sweater, with the dropped shoulders and round neck. It is knitted in an interesting variation on traditional Aran stitches: moss stitch and cable stitches worked to form 'cup' shapes. Knitted in cream it would look just like an Aran sweater and the stitch detail would show up beautifully, but it also looks good in bright colours or a useful navy.

MEASUREMENTS

To fit approx age
4–5(6:7–8:9) years.
Actual measurement
60.5(66:71:76.5)cm
(24(26:28:30)in).
Full length 33.5(36:38.5:41)cm
(13(14:15:16)in).
Sleeve seam 26(29:32:35)cm
(10¼(11½:12½:14)in).

MATERIALS

Rowan Cabled Mercerised Cotton
50g balls.
Navy (330) 5(6:7:8) balls.
Equivalent yarn: 3-ply.
1 pair each of 2¼mm (US 0) and
3mm (US 2) knitting needles.
Cable needle.
2 spare needles.

TENSION

30 sts and 38 rows to 10cm (4in)
on 3mm (US 2) needles over st st.
See page 10.

SPECIAL ABBREVIATIONS

T5L = sl next 2 sts onto CN and
leave at front of work, K2, then
P1, then K the 2 sts from CN.
T3B = sl next st onto CN and
leave at back of work, K next 2
sts, then P the st from CN.
T3F = sl next 2 sts onto CN and
leave at front of work, P next st,
then K the 2 sts from CN.

BACK

With 2¼mm (US 0) needles cast
on 88(96:104:112) sts and work in
K2, P2, rib for 5cm (2in).
Inc row Rib and inc 27 sts evenly
across row. (115(123:131:139) sts)
Change to 3mm (US 2) needles
and work in patt as foll:
1st row (rs facing) P1(5:9:13),
K2, (P1, K1) twice, P1, K2, *P6,
T5L, P6, K2, (P1, K1) twice, P1,
K2, rep from * to last 1(5:9:13)
st(s), P to end.
2nd row K1(5:9:13), yf, sl 2, (P1,
K1) twice, P1, sl 2, yb, *K6, P2,
K1, P2, K6, yf, sl 2, (P1, K1)

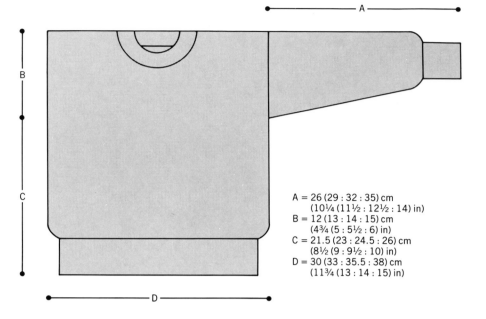

A = 26 (29 : 32 : 35) cm
    (10¼ (11½ : 12½ : 14) in)
B = 12 (13 : 14 : 15) cm
    (4¾ (5 : 5½ : 6) in)
C = 21.5 (23 : 24.5 : 26) cm
    (8½ (9 : 9½ : 10) in)
D = 30 (33 : 35.5 : 38) cm
    (11¾ (13 : 14 : 15) in)

twice, P1, sl 2, yb, rep from * to
last 1(5:9:13) st(s), K to end.
3rd row P1(5:9:13), K2, (P1, K1)
twice, P1, K2, *P5, T3B, K1,
T3F, P5, K2, (P1, K1) twice, P1,
K2, rep from * to last 1(5:9:13)
st(s), P to end.
4th row K1(5:9:13), yf, sl 2, (P1,
K1) twice, P1, sl 2, yb, *K5, P2,
K1, P1, K1, P2, K5, yf, sl 2, (P1,
K1) twice, P1, sl 2, yb, rep from *
to last 1(5:9:13) st(s), K to end.
5th row P1(5:9:13), K2, (P1, K1)
twice, P1, K2, *P4, T3B, K1, P1,
K1, T3F, P4, K2, (P1, K1) twice,
P1, K2, rep from * to last
1(5:9:13) st(s), P to end.
6th row K1(5:9:13), yf, sl 2, (P1,
K1) twice, P1, sl 2, yb, *K4, P2,
(K1, P1) twice, K1, P2, K4, yf,
sl 2, (P1, K1) twice, P1, sl 2, yb,
rep from * to last 1(5:9:13) st(s),
K to end.
7th row P1(5:9:13), K2, (P1, K1)
twice, P1, K2, *P3, T3B, (K1, P1)
twice, K1, T3F, P3, K2, (P1, K1)
twice, P1, K2, rep from * to last
1(5:9:13) st(s), P to end.
8th row K1(5:9:13), yf, sl 2, (P1,
K1) twice, P1, sl 2, yb, *K3, P2,
(K1, P1) 3 times, K1, P2, K3, yf,
sl 2, (P1, K1) twice, P1, sl 2, yb,
rep from * to last 1(5:9:13) st(s),
K to end.

9th row P1(5:9:13), K2, (P1, K1)
twice, P1, K2, *P2, T3B, (K1, P1)
3 times, K1, T3F, P2, K2, (P1,
K1) twice, P1, K2, rep from * to
last 1(5:9:13) st(s), P to end.
10th row K1(5:9:13), yf, sl 2, (P1,
K1) twice, P1, sl 2, yb, *K2, P2,
(K1, P1) 4 times, K1, P2, K2, yf,
sl 2, (P1, K1) twice, P1, sl 2, yb,
rep from * to last 1(5:9:13) st(s),
K to end.
11th row P1(5:9:13), K2, (P1,
K1) twice, P1, K2, *P1, T3B,
(K1, P1) 4 times, K1, T3F, P1,
K2, (P1, K1) twice, P1, K2,
rep from * to last 1 (5:9:13) st(s),
P to end.
12th row K1(5:9:13), yf, sl 2, (P1,
K1) twice, P1, sl 2, yb, *K1, P2,
(K1, P1) 5 times, K1, P2, K1, yf,
sl 2, (P1, K1) twice, P1, sl 2, yb,
rep from * to last 1(5:9:13) st(s),
K to end.
These 12 rows form the patt
and are rep as required. Cont
straight in patt as set until back
measures 33.5(36:38.5:41)cm
(13(14:15:16)in) from cast-on
edge, ending with a ws row.
Shape shoulders
Cast off 38(40:42:44) sts at beg of
next 2 rows.
Leave rem 39(43:47:51) sts on a
spare needle.

FRONT

Work as for back until front measures 28.5(30.5:32.5:34.5)cm (11¼(12:12¾:13½)in) from cast-on edge, ending with a ws row.

Shape front neck

Next row Patt 46(49:52:55), turn, work 2 tog, patt to end of row and work on this last set of 45(48:51:54) sts only.

**Keeping patt correct, dec 1 st at neck edge on every row until 38(40:42:44) sts rem.

Now cont straight until front measures same as back to cast-off shoulder edge, ending at side edge. Cast off.

Return to rem sts and sl centre 23(25:27:29) sts onto a spare needle, with rs facing rejoin yarn to rem sts and patt to end of row.

Next row Patt to last 2 sts, work 2 tog.

Now work as for first side from ** to end.

SLEEVES

With 2¼mm (US 0) needles cast on 40 sts and work in K2, P2, rib for 5cm (2in).

Inc row Rib and inc 11 sts evenly across row. (51 sts)

Change to 3mm (US 2) needles and work in patt as foll:

1st row (rs facing) P8, K2, (P1, K1) twice, P1, K2, P6, T5L, P6, K2, (P1, K1) twice, P1, K2, P8. The patt is now set. Cont in patt working as for back, *at the same time*, inc 1 st at both ends of every foll 4th row until there are 85(91:97:103) sts on the needle, working inc sts into reversed st st. Now cont straight until sleeve measures 26(29:32:35)cm (10¼ (11½:12½:14)in) from cast-on edge, ending with a ws row.

Cast off fairly loosely.

Rep patt for second sleeve.

NECKBAND

Join right shoulder seam.

With 2¼mm (US 0) needles and rs facing, pick up and K 19(22:23:26) sts down left front neck, K across centre front sts, pick up and K 19(22:23:26) sts up right front neck and finally K across centre back sts. (100(112:120:132) sts)

Work in K2, P2, rib for 7 rows.

Cast off loosely ribwise.

TO MAKE UP

Join left shoulder and neckband seam. With centre of cast-off edges of sleeves to shoulder seams, sew sleeves carefully in position reaching down to same depth on front and back. Join side and sleeve seams.

COTTON
FAIR ISLE

Cotton is not a traditional yarn for Fair Isles, but I started to use it because there are often more exciting or unusual shades to be found in cotton yarns. This style is very popular with all the men I know because of its casual, loose-fitting shape. The colours are useful because they go with practically everything, especially the cream, black or navy-blue trousers that men prefer.

MEASUREMENTS
To fit chest 97(102:107)cm
(38(40:42)in).
Actual measurement
110(115:120)cm
(43¼(45¼:47¼)in).
Full length 70(72:74)cm
(27½(28¼:29)in).
Sleeve seam 50(51:52)cm
(19¾(20:20½)in).

MATERIALS
Rowan Cabled Mercerised Cotton
50g balls.
Main colour (MC) navy (330)
6(7:7) balls;
1st contrast colour (A) granit
(325) 2(2:2) balls;
2nd contrast colour (B) cream
(301) 3(3:3) balls;
3rd contrast colour (C) olive (327)
2(2:2) balls;
4th contrast colour (D) thyme
(329) 2(2:2) balls;
5th contrast colour (E) souris
(318) 2(2:2) balls.
Equivalent yarn: 3-ply.
1 pair each of 2¼mm (US 0) and
3mm (US 2) knitting needles.
2 spare needles.

TENSION
34 sts and 36 rows to 10cm (4in)
on 3mm (US 2) needles over Fair
Isle patt. See page 10.

BACK
With 2¼mm (US 0) needles and
MC cast on 162(170:176) sts and
work in K1, P1, rib in the foll
stripe sequence:
3 rows MC, 3 rows A, 1 row B, 3
rows C, 1 row D, 2 rows E, 2 rows
C, 1 row B and 1 row A.
Now work a further 16 rows in rib,
but working backwards, ie start
with 1 row B, 2 rows C etc (33 rib
rows complete.)
Inc row Rib in MC and inc
26(26:28) sts evenly across row.
(188(196:204) sts)
Change to 3mm (US 2) needles
and starting with a K row work in

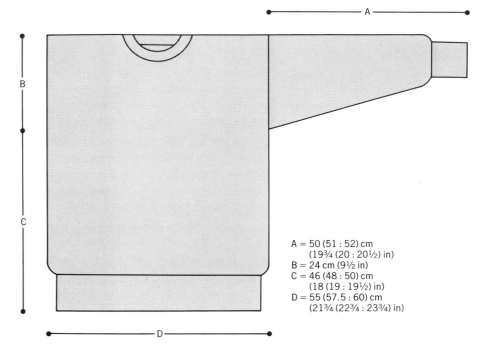

A = 50 (51 : 52) cm
  (19¾ (20 : 20½) in)
B = 24 cm (9½ in)
C = 46 (48 : 50) cm
  (18 (19 : 19½) in)
D = 55 (57.5 : 60) cm
  (21¾ (22¾ : 23¾) in)

st st from chart as foll:
1st row (rs facing) Work 4(2:0)
sts before the dotted line, rep the
12 st patt to last 4(2:0) sts, work
4(2:0) sts beyond the dotted line.
2nd row Work as 1st row.
Cont to work from chart as now
set, rep the 60 rows as required
until back measures 70(72:74)cm
(27½(28¼:29)in) from cast-on
edge, ending with a ws row.
Shape shoulders
Cast off 66(69:72) sts at beg of

next 2 rows.
Leave rem 56(58:60) sts on a
spare needle.

FRONT
Work as for back until front
measures 62(64:66)cm
(24½(25¼:26)in) from cast-on
edge, ending with a ws row.
Shape front neck
Next row Patt 81(84:87), turn,
work 2 tog, patt to end of row and
cont on this last set of 80(83:86)
sts only.
**Keeping patt correct, dec 1 st
at neck edge on every row until
66(69:72) sts rem.
Now cont straight until front
measures same as back to cast-off
shoulder edge ending at side edge.
Cast off.
Return to rem sts and sl centre
26(28:30) sts onto a spare needle,
with rs facing rejoin yarn to rem
sts and patt to end of row.
Next row Patt to last 2 sts, work
2 tog.
Now work as for first side from **
to end.

SLEEVES
With 2¼mm (US 0) needles and

MC, cast on 72(74:76) sts and
work in K1, P1, rib in stripe
sequence as for back welt for 33
rows.
Inc row Rib in MC and inc
24(22:20) sts evenly across row.
(96 sts)
Change to 3mm (US 2) needles
and starting with a K row work in
st st from chart, rep the 12 st patt
8 times across row.
Cont to work from chart, *at the
same time*, inc 1 st at both ends of
every foll 4th row until there are
162(164:166) sts on the needle,
working inc sts into patt.
Now cont straight until sleeve
measures 50(51:52)cm
(19¾(20:20½)in) from cast-on
edge, ending with a ws row.
Cast off fairly loosely.
Rep patt for second sleeve.

FAIR ISLE CHART

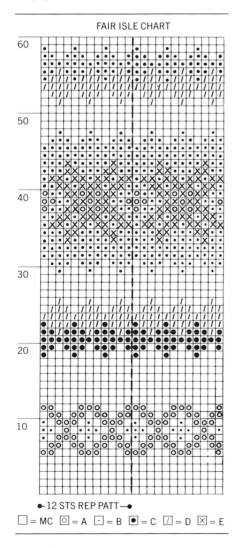

●–12 STS REP PATT–●

☐ = MC ◉ = A ⊡ = B ⚫ = C ⁄ = D ☒ = E

NECKBAND

Join right shoulder seam.
With 2¼mm (US 0) needles and
MC and rs facing, pick up and K
34 sts down left front neck, K
across centre front sts, pick up
and K 34 sts up right front neck
and finally K across centre back
sts. (150(154:158) sts)
Work in K1, P1, rib in the foll
stripe sequence:
1 row A, 1 row D, 1 row B, 1 row
E, 1 row C, 2 rows MC.
Cast off fairly loosely ribwise
using MC.

TO MAKE UP

Join left shoulder and neckband
seam. With centre of cast-off
edges of sleeves to shoulder seams,
sew sleeves carefully in position
reaching down to same patt row
on front and back. Join side and
sleeve seams matching patt.

TENNIS SWEATER

This is a real 1920's shape, perfect for an English afternoon tea on the lawn or a game of croquet. The contrast trim on the pockets, hem and V-neck gives it a sporty look but it could be made up without the trim if you prefer. It is quite an easy sweater to knit, in a simple cable pattern. The slim, lean shape looks good with a long pleated skirt.

MEASUREMENTS

To fit bust/chest
86–91(97:102:107)cm
(34–36(38:40:42)in).
Actual measurement
108(113:118:124)cm
(42½(44½:46½:49)in).
Full length 70(72.5:75:77.5)cm
(27½(28½:29½:30½)in).
Sleeve seam 45(46:47:48)cm
(17¾(18:18½:19)in).

MATERIALS

Rowan Cabled Mercerised Cotton
50g balls.
Main colour (MC) cream (301)
14(14:15:15) balls;
Contrast colour (C) navy (330)
1(1:1:1) ball.
Equivalent yarn: 3-ply.
1 pair each of 2¼mm (US 0) and
3mm (US 2) knitting needles.
One 2¼mm (US 0) circular
needle.
Cable needle.
3 spare needles.

TENSION

30 sts and 38 rows to 10cm (4in)
on 3mm (US 2) needles over st st.
See page 10.

SPECIAL ABBREVIATION

C2F = sl next 2 sts onto CN
and leave at front of work, K
next 2 sts, then K the 2 sts
from CN.

CABLE PANEL

Worked over 8 sts.
1st row (rs facing) P2, K4, P2.
2nd row K2, P4, K2.
Rep last 2 rows 4 times more.
11th row P2, C2F, P2.
12th row As 2nd row.
13th–20th rows As 1st and 2nd rows.
21st row As 11th row.
22nd row As 2nd row.
These 22 rows form the *cable panel* and are rep as required.

ZIG-ZAG MOSS STITCH PANEL

Worked over 18 sts.
1st row (rs facing) K2, (P1, K1) twice, P1, K11.
2nd row P10, (K1, P1) twice, K1, P3.
3rd row K4, (P1, K1) twice, P1, K9.
4th row P8, (K1, P1) twice, K1, P5.

5th row K6, (P1, K1) twice, P1, K7.
6th row P6, (K1, P1) twice, K1, P7.
7th row K8, (P1, K1) twice, P1, K5.
8th row P4, (K1, P1) twice, K1, P9.
9th row K10, (P1, K1) twice, P1, K3.
10th row P2, (K1, P1) twice, K1, P11.
11th row K12, (P1, K1) twice, P1, K1.
12th row As 10th row.
13th row As 9th row.
14th–20th rows As 8th–2nd rows (working in reverse order).
21st row K2, (P1, K1) twice, P1, K11.
22nd row P12, (K1, P1) twice, K1, P1.
These 22 rows form the *zig-zag panel* and are rep as required.

BACK

With 2¼mm (US 0) needles and MC, cast on 162(170:178:186) sts and work in K1, P1, rib for 6 rows.
Change to C and work 4 rows in rib as set.
Rep last 10 rows once more, then change to MC and work a further 6 rows in rib. (26 rib rows complete.)
Change to 3mm (US 2) needles and place patt as foll:
1st row (rs facing) K12(16:20:24), * work across 1st row of *cable panel*, work across 1st row of *zig-zag panel*, rep from * to last 20(24:28:32) sts, work across 1st row of *cable panel*, K12(16:20:24).
2nd row P12(16:20:24), *work 2nd row of *cable panel*, work 2nd row of *zig-zag panel*, rep from * to last 20(24:28:32) sts, work 2nd row of *cable panel*, P12(16:20:24).
Cont in patts as now set, rep the 22 rows of cable panel and zig-zag panel as required, and keeping side edges in st st until back

A = 45 (46 : 47 : 48) cm
(17¾ (18 : 18½ : 19) in)
B = 28 cm (11 in)
C = 45 (47.5 : 50 : 52.5) cm
(18 (18½ : 19½ : 20½) in)
D = 54 (56.5 : 59 : 62) cm
(21¼ (23¼ : 24½) in)

measures 70(72.5:75:77.5)cm (27½(28½:29½:30½)in) from cast-on edge, ending with a ws row.

Shape shoulders

Keeping patts correct, cast off 57(60:63:66) sts at beg of next 2 rows.

Leave rem 48(50:52:54) sts on a spare needle.

POCKET LININGS

With 3mm (US 2) needles and MC, cast on 44 sts and starting with a K row work in st st for 48 rows, thus ending with a ws row.

Leave sts on a spare needle.

Rep patt for second pocket lining.

FRONT

Work as for back until 48 rows of patt have been worked from top of rib.

Place pockets

Next row (rs facing) Patt 20(24:28:32), *sl next 44 sts on a spare needle and in their place patt across the 44 sts from first pocket lining*, patt next 34 sts, now work from * to * once more but working across sts of second pocket lining, patt to end of row.

Now cont in patt across the 162(170:178:186) sts until front measures 45(47.5:50:52.5)cm (17¾(18¾:19¾:20¾)in) from cast-on edge, ending with a ws row.

Shape front neck

Next row Patt 81(85:89:93), turn, work 2 tog, patt to end and work on this last set of 80(84:88:92) sts only.

**Keeping patt correct, dec 1 st at neck edge on every foll 3rd row until 57(60:63:66) sts rem.

Now cont straight until front measures same as back to cast-off shoulder edge, ending at side edge. Cast off all sts.

With rs facing rejoin yarn to rem 81(85:89:93) sts and patt to end of row.

Next row Patt to last 2 sts, work 2 tog.

Now work as for first side from ** to end.

SLEEVES

With 2¼mm (US 0) needles and MC, cast on 62 sts and work in K1, P1, rib and stripe sequence as for back welt for 25 rows.

Increase row With MC, rib and inc 38 sts evenly across row. (100 sts)

Change to 3mm (US 2) needles and place patt as foll:

1st row (rs facing) K20, * work across 1st row of *cable panel*, work across 1st row of *zig-zag panel*, rep from * once more, work across 1st row of *cable panel*, K20.

Cont in patts as now set, keeping side edges in st st, *at the same time*, inc 1 st at both ends of every foll 4th row until there are 170 sts on the needle, working inc sts into st st at either side.

Now cont straight until sleeve measures 45(46:47:48)cm (17¾(18:18½:19)in) from cast-on edge, ending with a ws row.

Cast off fairly loosely.

Rep patt for second sleeve.

NECKBAND

Join right shoulder seam carefully matching patts.

With the 2¼mm (US 0) circular needle and MC and rs facing pick up and K 90(94:98:102) sts down left front neck, pick up and K a thread at centre front, then pick up and K 90(94:98:102) sts up right front neck and finally K across back neck sts. (229(239:249:259) sts)

Work in *rows* of K1, P1, rib for 3 rows, dec 1 st at either side of centre front st on each row.

Change to C and work 4 rows in rib as set, dec at centre front as before.

Change to MC and work 2 rows in rib as set, dec at centre front as before.

Cast off fairly loosely ribwise, dec as before.

POCKET TOPS

With 2¼mm (US 0) needles and rs facing, work in K1, P1, rib across the 44 sts on one spare needle in same stripe sequence as for neckband.

Cast off fairly loosely ribwise.

TO MAKE UP

Join left shoulder and neckband seam. With centre of cast-off edges of sleeves to shoulder seams, sew sleeves carefully in position, reaching down to same depth on front and back. Join side and sleeve seams, matching stripes. Catch down side edges of pocket tops and sl st pocket linings neatly in position on wrong side.

HUNGARIAN CARDIGAN

The fitted shape of this cardigan is very flattering and the sparkling buttons take it beautifully from day to evening. It was inspired by my collection of Hungarian gypsy costumes from the late nineteenth and early twentieth century. Hungarian women embroider all their clothes elaborately: aprons, blouses, sleeves and the hems of their skirts. They always use strong, bright colours co-ordinated in ways that might not be immediately obvious, but with striking results. I find their use of elaborate floral patterns particularly inspiring.

MEASUREMENTS

To fit bust 81–86(91:97)cm
(32–34(36:38)in).
Actual measurement
92(97:104)cm (36¼(38:41)in).
Full length 60(63:66)cm
(23½(24¾:26)in).
Sleeve seam 46cm (18in).

MATERIALS

Rowan Lightweight D.K. Wool
25g hanks.
Main colour (MC) black (62)
23(24:24) hanks;
1st contrast colour (A) green
(606) 1(1:1) hank;
2nd contrast colour (B) mustard
(72) 1(1:1) hank.
Rowan Fine Cotton Chenille
50g balls (used double).
3rd contrast colour (C) cyclamen
(385) 1(1:1) ball;
4th contrast colour (D) purple
(384) 1(1:1) ball;
5th contrast colour (E) cardinal
(379) 1(1:1) ball;
6th contrast colour (F) mole (380)
1(1:1) ball.
Equivalent yarn: D.K. used
throughout.
1 pair each of 2¾mm (US 1) and
3¼mm (US 3) knitting needles.
10 buttons.

TENSION

26 sts and 34 rows to 10cm (4in)
on 3¼mm (US 3) needles over
st st using MC. See page 10.

RIGHT FRONT

With 2¾mm (US 1) needles and
MC, cast on 64(72:76) sts and
work in K2, P2, rib for 2.5cm
(1in), inc 2 sts across row on *1st
and 3rd sizes only.* (66(72:78) sts)**
Change to 3¼mm (US 3) needles
and starting with a K row work in
st st from *right front chart.* Dec 1 st
at side edge on 4th row, and then
rows as indicated until 43(51:57)
sts rem. Work 9 rows straight,
then inc 1 st at side edge on next
row and then rows as indicated

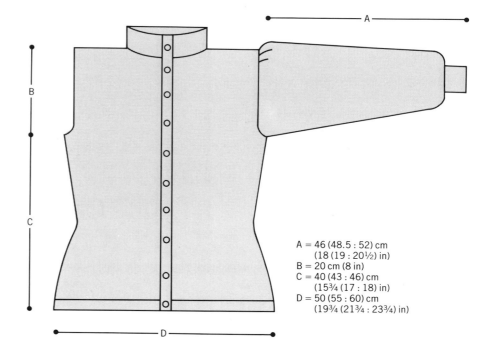

A = 46 (48.5 : 52) cm
    (18 (19 : 20½) in)
B = 20 cm (8 in)
C = 40 (43 : 46) cm
    (15¾ (17 : 18) in)
D = 50 (55 : 60) cm
    (19¾ (21¾ : 23¾) in)

until there are 58(64:70) sts on
the needle. Now work 4(5:5)
rows straight, thus ending at
side edge.

Shape armhole

Cast off 6 sts at side edge on next
row, then dec 1 st at this edge on
foll 7(9:11) rows. (45(49:53) sts)
Now cont straight until
168th(180th:192nd) row of chart
has been worked.

Shape front neck

Cast off 10 sts at beg (neck edge)
on next row, then dec 1 st at this
edge on every row 9 times.
(26(30:34) sts)
Now cont straight until
192nd(204th:216th) row of chart
has been worked.
Cast off.

LEFT FRONT

Work as for right front to **.
Change to 3¼mm (US 3) needles
and starting with a P row work in
st st from *right front chart* (this
reverses chart and front).
Complete as for right front,
working odd numbered rows as
P rows (reading from right to left)
and even numbered rows as K
rows (reading from left to right).

BACK

With 2¾mm (US 1) needles
and MC, cast on 132(144:156) sts
and work in K2, P2, rib for
2.5cm (1in).
Change to 3¼mm (US 3) needles
and starting with a K row work in
st st from *back border chart.* When
the 16 rows of chart have been
worked, cont in st st in MC only
for a further 10(18:24) rows.

Shape waist

Next row (rs facing) K.
Next row P.
Next row *K5, K2 tog, K5, rep
from * to end. (121(132:143) sts)
Starting with a P row work 5 rows
in st st.
Next row *K5, K2 tog, K4, rep
from * to end. (110(120:130) sts)
Starting with a P row work 5 rows
in st st.
Next row *K4, K2 tog, K4, rep
from * to end. (99(108:117) sts)
Starting with a P row work 5 rows
in st st.
Next row *K4, K2 tog, K3, rep
from * to end. (88(96:104) sts)
Starting with a P row work 5 rows
in st st.
Next row *K3, K2 tog, K3, rep
from * to end. (77(84:91) sts)

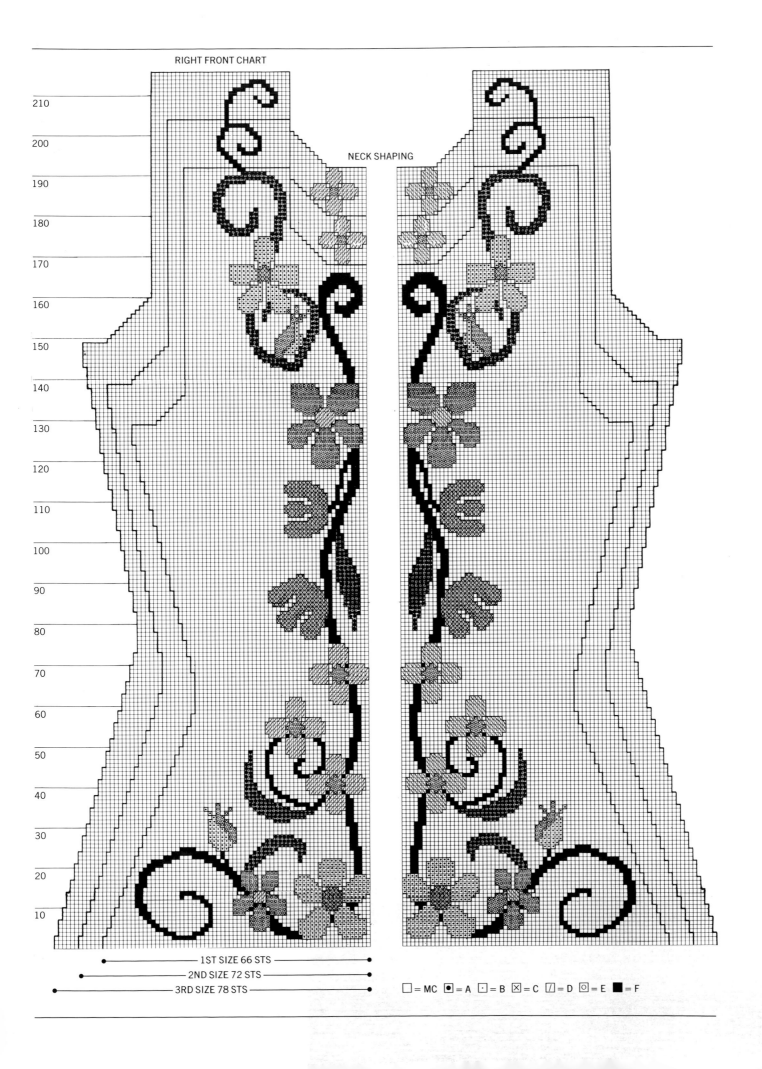

RIGHT FRONT CHART

NECK SHAPING

210
200
190
180
170
160
150
140
130
120
110
100
90
80
70
60
50
40
30
20
10

● 1ST SIZE 66 STS ●
● 2ND SIZE 72 STS ●
● 3RD SIZE 78 STS ●

□ = MC ● = A · = B ⊠ = C ⁄ = D ◎ = E ■ = F

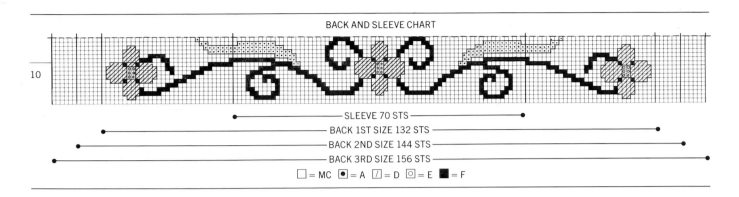

BACK AND SLEEVE CHART

10

SLEEVE 70 STS
BACK 1ST SIZE 132 STS
BACK 2ND SIZE 144 STS
BACK 3RD SIZE 156 STS

□ = MC   ● = A   ⁄ = D   ○ = E   ■ = F

Starting with a P row work in st st for 12 rows.

Now cont in st st and inc 1 st at both ends of every foll 3rd row until there are 119(126:135) sts on the needle.

Now work a few rows straight until 128(138:148) rows of st st have been worked from top of rib, thus ending with a ws row.

Shape armholes

Cast off 7 sts at beg of next 2 rows. Now dec 1 st at both ends of every row until 97(104:113) sts rem. Cont straight until back measures 8 rows shorter than fronts to cast-off shoulder edge, thus ending with a ws row.

Shape back neck

Next row K 33(37:41), cast off centre 31(30:31) sts, K to end of row and work on this last set of sts only.

***Dec 1 st at neck edge on every row until 26(30:34) sts rem, and back measures same as front to cast-off shoulder edge. Cast off. With ws facing rejoin yarn to rem sts and work as for first side from *** to end.

SLEEVES

With 2¾mm (US 1) needles and MC cast on 56 sts and work in K2, P2, rib for 5cm (2in), inc 14 sts evenly across last row. (70 sts) Change to 3¼mm (US 3) needles and starting with a K row work in st st from *back border chart*, working between sts as indicated for sleeves.

When the 16 rows of chart have been worked, cont in MC only, now inc 1 st at both ends of every foll 4th row until there are 120 sts on the needle.

Now cont straight until sleeve measures 46cm (18in) from cast-on edge, ending with a ws row.

Shape top

Cast off 10 sts at beg of next 2 rows.

Now dec 1 st at both ends of every row until 60 sts rem.

Now cast off 3 sts at beg of next 16 rows. (12 sts)

Cast off rem sts.

Rep patt for second sleeve.

TO MAKE UP

Join both shoulder seams.

Join side and sleeve seams. Set sleeves into armholes, gathering fullness evenly across top of shoulders.

BUTTONHOLE BAND

With 2¾mm (US 1) needles and MC and rs facing, pick up and K 136(140:144) sts evenly up right front. Work in K2, P2, rib for 3 rows.

Buttonhole row (rs facing) Rib 2(4:6), *cast off 2 sts, rib 14, rep from * to last 6(8:10) sts, cast off 2 sts, rib to end.

Next row Rib, casting on 2 sts over cast-off sts on previous row. (9 buttonholes worked.)

Work a further 2 rows in rib.

Cast off loosely ribwise.

BUTTON BAND

Work as for buttonhole band, picking up sts down left front, and working in P2, K2, rib as for buttonhole band but omitting buttonholes.

Cast off loosely ribwise.

NECKBAND

With 2¾mm (US 1) needles and MC and rs facing, pick up and K 40 sts up right front neck, including top of buttonhole band, 60 sts across back neck, and 40 sts down left front neck including top of button band. (140 sts)

Work in K2, P2, rib for 2.5cm (1in), ending with a ws row.

Buttonhole row Rib 4 sts, cast off 2 sts, rib to end.

Next row Rib, casting on 2 sts over cast-off sts on previous row.

Cont in rib until neckband measures 7.5cm (3in), then rep the 2 buttonhole rows once more.

Work a further 2.5cm (1in) in rib.

Cast off fairly loosely ribwise.

Fold neckband in half to inside and sl st neatly in position sewing around buttonhole. Sew on buttons to correspond with buttonholes.

CLASSIC FAIR ISLE

Knitters in the Shetland Islands of Scotland originally designed Fair Isles to use up their leftover pieces of yarn. The number of colour changes can make them quite fiddly to knit. I have chosen a very traditional 1930's colourway for this sweater, which is especially popular with American visitors to London and which also suits the classic Fair Isle shape of the garment.

MEASUREMENTS

To fit chest 86(91:97:102:107)cm
(34(36:38:40:42)in).
Actual measurement
105(111:116:122:127)cm
(41¼(43¾:45¾:48:50)in).
Full length 68(70:72:74:76)cm
(26¾(27½:28¼:29:29¾)in).
Sleeve seam 50(51:52:53:54)cm
(19¾(20:20½:21:21¼)in).

MATERIALS

Rowan Lightweight D.K. Wool
25g hanks.
Main colour (MC) light beige
(613) 20(20:20:21:21) hanks;
1st contrast colour (A) black (62)
1(1:1:2:2) hank(s);
2nd contrast colour (B) leaf green
(407) 1(1:1:2:2) hank(s);
3rd contrast colour (C) maroon
(45) 5(5:5:6:6) hanks;
4th contrast colour (D) green
(606) 5(5:5:6:6) hanks;
5th contrast colour (E) mist (77)
2(2:2:3:3) hanks;
6th contrast colour (F) beige (86)
2(2:2:3:3) hanks;
7th contrast colour (G) navy (97)
2(2:2:3:3) hanks;
8th contrast colour (H) nut (71)
1(1:1:2:2) hank(s).
Equivalent yarn: D.K.
1 pair each of 2¾mm (US 1) and
3¼mm (US 3) knitting needles.
2 spare needles.

TENSION

29 sts and 30 rows to 10cm (4in)
on 3¼mm (US 3) needles over
Fair Isle patt. See page 10.

BACK

With 2¼mm (US 1) needles and
MC, cast on 140(148:156:
164:172) sts and work in K1, P1,
rib for 10cm (4in).
Inc row Rib and inc 13 sts
evenly across row.
(153(161:169:177:185) sts)
Change to 3¼mm (US 3) needles
and starting with a K row work in
st st from chart as foll:

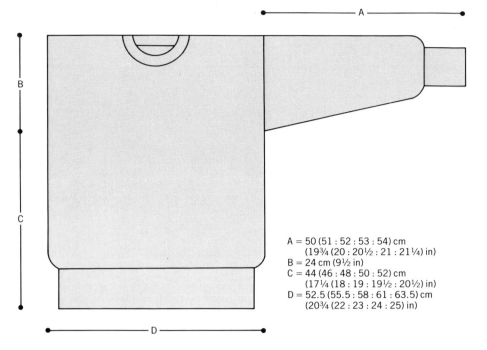

A = 50 (51 : 52 : 53 : 54) cm
(19¾ (20 : 20½ : 21 : 21¼) in)
B = 24 cm (9½ in)
C = 44 (46 : 48 : 50 : 52) cm
(17¼ (18 : 19 : 19½ : 20½) in)
D = 52.5 (55.5 : 58 : 61 : 63.5) cm
(20¾ (22 : 23 : 24 : 25) in)

1st row (rs facing) Work 4(2:0:4:2)
sts before the dotted line, rep
the 12 st patt 12(13:14:14:15) times
across, work 5(3:1:5:3) st(s)
beyond the dotted line.
2nd row Work 5(3:1:5:3) st(s)
before the dotted line, rep the 12
st patt 12(13:14:14:15) times
across, work 4(2:0:4:2) sts beyond
the dotted line.
Cont in patt as now set, rep the 76
rows of chart as required until
back measures 68(70:72:74:76)cm
(26¾(27½:28¼:29:29¾)in) from
cast-on edge, ending with a ws
row.
Shape shoulders
Cast off 53(56:59:62:65) sts at beg
of next 2 rows.
Leave rem 47(49:51:53:55) sts on
a spare needle.

FRONT

Work as for back until front
measures 60(62:64:66:68)cm
(23½(24¼:25¼:26:26¾)in) from
cast-on edge, ending with a ws
row.
Shape front neck
Next row Patt 63(66:69:72:75),
turn, work 2 tog, patt to end and
work on this last set of

62(65:68:71:74) sts only.
****Keeping patt correct, dec 1 st
at neck edge on every row until
53(56:59:62:65) sts rem.
Now cont straight until front
measures same as back to cast-off
shoulder edge, ending at side
edge. Cast off.
Return to rem sts and sl centre
27(29:31:33:35) sts onto a spare
needle, with rs facing, rejoin yarn
to rem sts and patt to end of row.
Next row Patt to last 2 sts, work
2 tog.
Now work as for first side from **
to end.

SLEEVES

With 2¾mm (US 1) needles and
MC, cast on 66(68:70:72:74) sts
and work in K1, P1, rib for 10cm
(4in).
Inc row Rib and inc
31(29:27:25:23) sts evenly across
row. (97 sts)
Change to 3¼mm (US 3) needles
and starting with a K row work in
st st from chart as foll:
1st row (rs facing) Work the 12 st
patt 8 times across row, work 1 st
beyond dotted line.
2nd row Work 1 st before dotted

line, rep the 12 st patt 8 times
across.

The patt is now set. Cont to rep
the 76 rows of chart, *at the same
time*, inc 1 st at both ends of every
foll 5th row until there are
141(143,145,145,147) sts on the
needle, working inc sts into patt.
Now cont straight until sleeve
measures 50(51:52:53:54)cm
(19¾(20:20½:21:21¼)in) from
cast-on edge, ending with a ws
row.

Cast off loosely.

Rep patt for second sleeve.

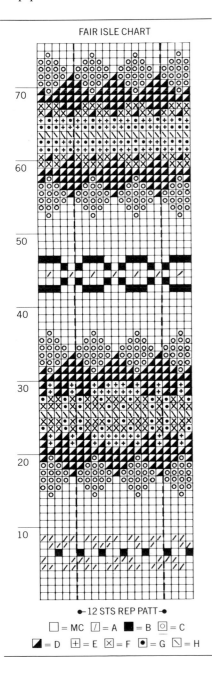

FAIR ISLE CHART

●–12 STS REP PATT–●

☐ = MC ⧄ = A ■ = B ⊡ = C

◪ = D ⊞ = E ⊠ = F ⊙ = G ◩ = H

NECKBAND

Join right shoulder seam.
With 2¾mm (US 1) needles and
MC and rs facing, pick up and K
30 sts down left front neck, K
across centre front sts, pick up
and K 30 sts up right front neck
and finally K across centre back
sts. (134(138,142,146,150) sts)
Work in K1, P1, rib for 7 rows.

Cast off loosely ribwise.

TO MAKE UP

Join left shoulder and neckband
seam. With centre of cast-off
edges of sleeves to shoulder seams,
new sleeves carefully in position
reaching down to same patt row
on front and back. Join side and
sleeve seams, matching patts.

FAN BOBBLE
SWEATER

This romantic classic style was adapted from an original 1940's sweater that I was particularly fond of. The fan bobble stitch is a traditional 1940's one in which rows of bobbles are formed into fan shapes. If you like, the bobbles could be replaced with beads. The fitted waist and luxurious silk yarn make it a very elegant sweater for evening wear and it would also look good in bright colours such as fuchsia.

MEASUREMENTS

To fit bust 81–86 (97–102)cm
(32–34(38–40)in).
Actual measurement 90(104)cm
(35½(41)in).
Full length 65cm (25½in).
Sleeve seam 45cm (17¾in).

MATERIALS

Rowan Mulberry Silk 50g hanks.
Fondant (878) 15(16) hanks.
Equivalent yarn: 4-ply.
1 pair each of 2mm (US 00) and
3mm (US 2) knitting needles.
One 2mm (US 00) short circular
needle.
2 spare needles.

TENSION

28 sts and 36 rows to 10cm (4in)
on 3mm (US 2) needles over st st.
See page 10.

NOTE

When working in patt, st count
varies on some rows. *This must be
taken into account* when counting sts
during shaping. St counts given
during shapings always refer to
the original number of sts.

BACK

With 3mm (US 2) needles cast on
128(146) sts and work in K1, P1,
rib for 3cm (1¼in).
Now work in patt as foll:
1st row (rs facing) Sl 1, *K into
front and back of next st, (knit
into front and back of next st 3
times (making 6 sts) now sl first 5
sts over last st, thus making a
bobble, P3) 4 times, K into front
and back of next st 3 times, sl first
5 sts over last st, sl last st back
onto left-hand needle and K into
front and back of it, rep from * to
last st, K1. (142(162) sts)
2nd row Sl 1, *P2, (K3, P1) 4
times, P2, rep from * to last st,
K1.
3rd row Sl 1, *K1, K twice into
next st, (K1, P3) 4 times, K twice
into next st, K1, rep from * to last

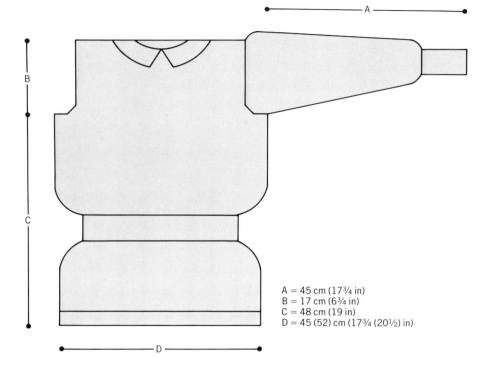

A = 45 cm (17¾ in)
B = 17 cm (6¾ in)
C = 48 cm (19 in)
D = 45 (52) cm (17¾ (20½) in)

st, K1. (156(178) sts)
4th row Sl 1, *P3, (K3, P1) 4
times, P3, rep from * to last st,
K1.
5th row Sl 1, *K2, K twice into
next st, (K1, P3) 4 times, K twice
into next st, K2, rep from * to last
st, K1. (170(194) sts)
6th row Sl 1, *P4, (K3, P1) 4
times, P4, rep from * to last st,
K1.
7th row Sl 1, *K3, K twice into
next st, (K1, P2 tog, P1) 4 times,
K twice into next st, K3, rep from
* to last st, K1. (156(178) sts)
8th row Sl 1, *P5, (K2, P1) 4
times, P5, rep from * to last st,
K1.
9th row Sl 1, *K4, K twice into
next st, (K1, P2 tog) 4 times, K
twice into next st, K4, rep from *
to last st, K1. (142(162) sts)
10th row Sl 1, *P6, (K1, P1) 4
times, P6, rep from * to last st,
K1.
11th row Sl 1, *K5, K twice into
next st, K1, (K2 tog) 3 times, take
next 2 sts tog, K into front and
then into back of them, K5, rep
from * to last st, K1.
(128(146) sts)

12th row Sl 1, P to last st, K1.
These 12 rows form the patt and
are rep as required.
Rep these 12 rows 4 times more.
(60 patt rows worked.)
Change to 2mm (US 00) needles
and work in K1, P1, rib for 6cm
(2½in).
Change to 3mm (US 2) needles
and starting with a 1st row work
in patt as before, *at the same time*,
inc 1 st at both ends of every foll
7th row until there are 140(160)
sts on the needle, working inc sts
into st st.
Now cont straight until 7
complete patts have been worked
from top of waist ribbing, thus
ending with a ws row. (84 patt
rows.)
Shape armholes
Cast off 10(12) sts at beg of next
2 rows.
Now cast off 6(8) sts at beg of foll
2 rows. (108(120) sts)
Now work straight until 12½
patts have been worked from top
of waist ribbing, ending with a ws
row. (150 patt rows.)
Shape shoulders
Cast off 34(36) sts at beg of next

2 rows.
Leave rem sts on a spare needle.

FRONT

Work as for back, shaping armholes as for back, until the 10th patt from waist ribbing has been worked, thus ending with a ws row. (120 patt rows.)

Shape front neck

Next row Patt 43(47), sl next 22(26) sts on a spare needle, patt to end of row and work on this last set of sts only.

**Keeping patt correct as far as possible, dec 1 st at neck edge on every row until 34(36) sts rem. Now cont straight until front measures same as back to cast-off shoulder edge, ending at armhole edge. Cast off.

With ws facing rejoin yarn to rem sts and work as for first side from ** to end.

SLEEVES

With 2mm (US 00) needles cast on 62 sts and work in K1, P1, rib for 10cm (4in).

Inc row Rib and inc 30 sts evenly across row. (92 sts)

Change to 3mm (US 2) needles and work in patt as for back, *at the same time*, inc 1 st at both ends of every foll 6th row until there are 104 sts on the needle, working inc sts into st st.

Now cont straight until sleeve measures 45cm (17¾in) from cast-on edge, ending with a ws row.

Shape top

Cast off 4 sts at beg of next 2 rows. Keeping patt correct, dec 1 st at both ends of every foll alt row until 50 sts rem.

Now dec 1 st at both ends of every row until 24 sts rem.
Cast off.
Rep patt for second sleeve.

COLLAR

Join both shoulder seams.

With the 2mm (US 00) circular needle and rs facing, pick up and K 26 sts down left front neck, K across centre front sts, pick up and K 26 sts up right front neck and finally K across centre back sts.

Work in rounds of K1, P1, rib for 6 rounds, ending at centre front.

Divide for collar

Next row Rib to centre front, turn, and work backwards and forwards in rows of K1, P1, rib until collar measures 8cm (3in) from division.

Cast off loosely ribwise.

TO MAKE UP

Join side and sleeve seams. Set sleeves into armholes, gathering fullness evenly across top of shoulder. Turn collar to right side.

ABSTRACT FLORAL SWEATER

I wanted to design a sweater that mixed abstract with flower patterns but without being overly floral, and this is the result. Because the flowers are worked in chenille against a cotton background, they stand out and look very textural. The pattern also looks good against a dusky beige background. Selina Scott bought the cardigan version.

MEASUREMENTS

One size only to fit bust 86–102cm (34–40in).
Actual measurement 126cm (49½in).
Full length 73cm (28¾in).
Sleeve seam 47cm (18½in).

MATERIALS

Rowan Handknit D.K. Cotton 50g balls.
Main colour (MC) ecru (251) 17 balls.
Rowan Fine Cotton Chenille 50g balls (used double).
1st contrast colour (A) lacquer (388) 2 balls.
Rowan Cotton Chenille 100g hanks.
2nd contrast colour (B) black (367) 2 hanks;
3rd contrast colour (C) fern (364) 1 hank;
4th contrast colour (D) french mustard (363) 1 hank.
Equivalent yarn: D.K. used throughout.
1 pair each of 3¾mm (US 4) and 4mm (US 5) knitting needles.
One 3¾mm (US 4) short circular needle.
2 spare needles.

TENSION

20 sts and 28 rows to 10cm (4in) on 4mm (US 5) needles over st st using MC. See page 10.

BACK

With 3¾mm (US 4) needles and MC, cast on 116 sts and work in K2, P2, rib for 5cm (2in).
Change to 4mm (US 5) needles and starting with a K row work in st st and place charts as foll:
1st row (rs facing) Work across the 29 sts of 1st row of *chart 1*, 4 times.
Cont as now set until 12th row of chart has been worked.
Next row (rs facing) Patt across the 58 sts of 1st row of *chart 2*, now patt across the 29 sts of 1st row

of *chart 1* twice.
Next row Patt across the 29 sts of 2nd row of *chart 1* twice, now patt across the 58 sts of 2nd row of *chart 2*.
Cont to work charts as now placed until the 34 rows of each chart are complete, *at the same time*, inc 1 st at both ends of 10th and 32nd rows. (120 sts)
Next row (rs facing) K2MC, now patt across the 29 sts of 1st row of *chart 1*, patt across the 58 sts of 1st row of *chart 2*, then patt across the 29 sts of 1st row of *chart 1*, K2MC.
Next row P2MC, patt across the 29 sts of 2nd row of *chart 1*, patt across the 58 sts of 2nd row of *chart 2*, then patt across the 29 sts of 2nd row of *chart 1*, P2MC.
Cont to work charts as now placed until the 34 rows of each chart are complete, *at the same time*, inc 1 st at both ends of 20th row. (122 sts)
Next row (rs facing) K3MC, now work across the 29 sts of 1st row of *chart 1*, 4 times, K3MC.
Next row P3MC, now work across the 29 sts of 2nd row of *chart 1*, 4 times, P3MC.
Cont to work chart as now placed until the 34th row of chart is

complete, *at the same time*, inc 1 st at both ends of 8th and 30th rows. (126 sts)
Shape armholes
Next row (rs facing) Cast off 5 sts, patt across the 29 sts of 1st row of *chart 1* twice, patt across the 58 sts of 1st row of *chart 2*, K5MC.
Next row Cast off 5 sts, patt across the 58 sts of 2nd row of *chart 2*, now patt across the 29 sts of 2nd row of *chart 1* twice. (116 sts)
Cont to work charts as now placed until the 34 rows of each chart are complete.
Next row (rs facing) Patt across the 58 sts of 1st row of *chart 2*, then patt across the 29 sts of 1st row of *chart 1* twice.
Next row Patt across the 29 sts of 2nd row of *chart 1* twice, then patt across the 58 sts of 2nd row of *chart 2*.
Cont to work charts as now placed until the 26th row of each chart has been worked.
Shape back neck
Next row (rs facing – 27th row of charts) Patt 45, sl next 26 sts onto a spare needle, patt to end and cont on this last set of 45 sts only.

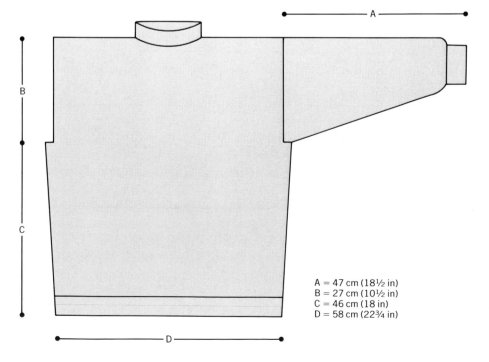

A = 47 cm (18½ in)
B = 27 cm (10½ in)
C = 46 cm (18 in)
D = 58 cm (22¾ in)

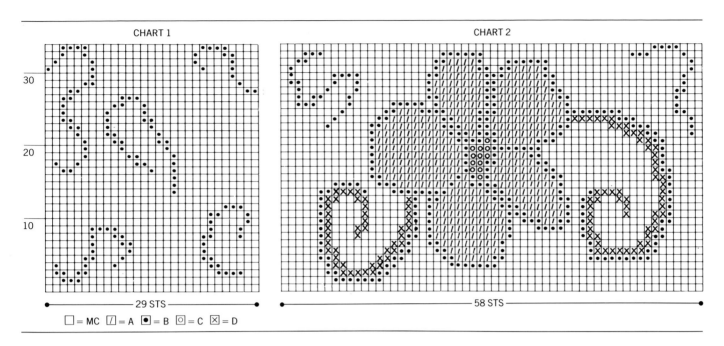

CHART 1   CHART 2

— 29 STS —   — 58 STS —

□ = MC   ☑ = A   ◉ = B   ◎ = C   ☒ = D

**Keeping patts correct, dec 1 st at neck edge on every row until 38 sts rem and the 34th row of chart is complete.
Cast off.
With ws facing rejoin yarn to rem sts and work as for first side from ** to end.

FRONT
Work as for back until the 20th row of last line of charts has been worked.
Shape front neck
Next row (rs facing) Patt 45, sl next 26 sts onto a spare needle, patt to end and cont on this last set of 45 sts only.
***Keeping patts correct, dec 1 st at neck edge on every row until 38 sts rem.
Now cont straight until front measures same as back to cast-off shoulder edge, ending with same patt row.
Cast off.
With ws facing rejoin yarn to rem sts and work as for first side from *** to end.

SLEEVES
With 3¾mm (US 4) needles and MC, cast on 56 sts and work in K2, P2, rib for 5cm (2in), and inc

1 st at both ends of last row only. (58 sts)
Change to 4mm (US 5) needles and starting with a K row work in st st and place charts as foll:
1st row (rs facing) Work across the 29 sts of 1st row of *chart 1* twice.
Cont to work chart as now placed until the 34 rows of chart are complete, *at the same time*, inc 1 st at both ends of 6th row and then every foll 4th row.
Next row (rs facing – 74 sts) K8MC, now work across the 58 sts of 1st row of *chart 2*, K8MC.
Next row P8MC, now work across the 58 sts of 2nd row of *chart 2*, P8MC.
Cont to work chart as now placed until the 34 rows of chart are complete, cont to inc at both ends of every foll 4th row as before.
Next row (rs facing – 90 sts) K2MC, now work across the 29 sts of 1st row of *chart 1*, 3 times, K1MC.
Next row P1MC, now work across the 29 sts of 2nd row of *chart 1*, 3 times, P2MC.
Cont to work chart as now placed until the 34 rows are complete, cont to inc at both ends of every foll 4th row as before.

Next row (rs facing – 108 sts) K in MC
Next row P in MC.
Cast off fairly loosely in MC.
Rep patt for second sleeve.

NECKBAND
Join both shoulder seams.
With the 3¾mm (US 4) circular needle and rs facing and MC, pick up and K 92 sts evenly around neck edge, including sts on spare needles.
Work in rounds of K2, P2, rib for 8cm (3in).
Cast off fairly loosely ribwise.

TO MAKE UP
Fold neckband in half to inside and sl st loosely in position.
With centre of cast-off edges of sleeves to shoulder seams, sew sleeves into armholes, sewing top half of sleeves to cast-off sts at armholes. Join side and sleeve seams.

FISHERMAN'S ARAN

Any man would love this straightforward chunky Aran sweater, which looks good knitted in navy, as here, or in cream, as you can see in the photograph on page 69. Originally fishing sweaters, Arans come from the Aran Islands in the mouth of the Galway Bay, off the west coast of Ireland. Aran knitting, like Fair Isle, is a traditional craft which I am very keen to keep alive.

MEASUREMENTS
To fit bust/chest
86–97(102–112)cm
(34–38(40–44)in).
Actual measurement 110(122)cm
(43¼(48)in).
Full length 65(68)cm
(25½(26¾)in).
Sleeve seam 43(45)cm
(17(17¾)in).

MATERIALS
Rowan Handknit D.K. Cotton
50g balls.
Turkish plum (277) or ecru (251)
24(25) balls.
Equivalent yarn: D.K.
1 pair each of 3¾mm (US 4) and
4mm (US 5) knitting needles.
One 3¾mm (US 4) circular
needle.
Cable needle.
Safety pin.

TENSION
20 sts and 28 rows to 10cm (4in)
on 4mm (US 5) needles over st st.
See page 10.

SPECIAL ABBREVIATIONS
FCrP = sl next 2 sts onto CN and
leave at front of work, P next st,
then K the 2 sts from CN.
BCr = sl next st onto CN and
leave at back of work, K next 2
sts, then P the st from CN.
C2F = sl next 2 sts onto CN and
leave at front of work, K next 2
sts, then K the 2 sts from CN.
MB = make bobble by (K1, P1)
into next 2 sts, turn, P4, turn, K4,
turn, P4, turn and (K2 tog) twice.
Cr2B = sl next 3 sts onto CN and
leave at back of work, K next 2
sts, then sl P st from CN back to
left-hand needle and P it, then K
rem 2 sts from CN.

PANEL A
Worked over a multiple of 2 sts
plus 1.
1st row (rs facing) P1, *K1, P1,
rep from * to end.

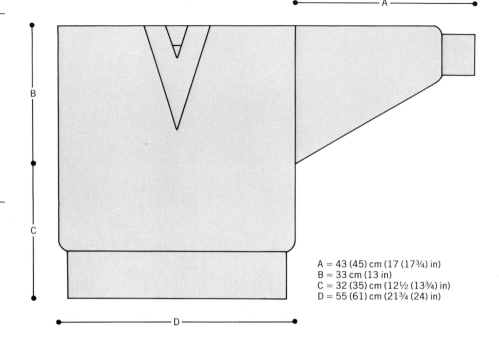

A = 43 (45) cm (17 (17¾) in)
B = 33 cm (13 in)
C = 32 (35) cm (12½ (13¾) in)
D = 55 (61) cm (21¾ (24) in)

2nd row P1, *K1, P1, rep from *
to end.
These 2 rows form *panel A* and are
rep as required.

PANEL B
Worked over 7 sts.
1st row (rs facing) P1, K5, P1.
2nd row K1, P5, K1.
Rep last 2 rows once more.
5th row P7.
6th row As 2nd row.
These 6 rows form *panel B* and are
rep as required.

PANEL C
Worked over 7 sts.
1st row (rs facing) FCrP, P4.
2nd row and every foll ws row
K all K sts and P all P sts.
3rd row K1, FCrP, P3.
5th row P1, K1, FCrP, P2.
7th row K1, P1, K1, FCrP, P1.
9th row (P1, K1) twice, FCrP.
11th row (K1, P1) twice, BCr.
13th row P1, K1, P1, BCr, P1.
15th row K1, P1, BCr, P2.
17th row P1, BCr, P3.
19th row BCr, P4.
20th row As 2nd row.
These 20 rows form *panel C* and
are rep as required.

PANEL D
Worked over 8 sts.
1st row (rs facing) K1B, P1, K4,
P1, K1B.
2nd row and every foll ws row
P1, K1, P4, K1, P1.
3rd row K1B, P1, C2F, P1, K1B.
5th and 7th rows As 1st row.
8th row As 2nd row.
These 8 rows form *panel D* and are
rep as required.

PANEL E
Worked over 8 sts.
1st–4th rows Starting with a K
row work 4 rows in st st.
5th row (rs facing) K3, MB, K3.
6th–10th rows Starting with a P
row work 5 rows in st st.
Rep rows *5–10 only* for *panel E* and
these 6 rows are rep as required.

PANEL F
Worked over 12 sts.
1st row (rs facing) P4, K4, P4.
2nd row K4, P1, sl 2, P1, K4.
3rd row P2, sl next 3 sts onto CN
and hold at back of work, K1,
then P1, K1, P1, from CN. Sl
next st onto CN and hold at front
of work, K1, P1, K1, then K1
from CN, P2.

4th row K2, (P1, K1) 3 times, P2, K2.

5th row P2, (K1, P1) 3 times, K2, P2.

6th–9th rows As 4th and 5th rows.

10th row K2, sl 1 with yf, (K1, P1) 3 times, sl 1 with yf, K2.

11th row P2, sl next st onto CN and hold at front of work, P2, K1, then K1 from CN. Sl next 3 sts onto CN and hold at

back of work, K1, then K1, P2, from CN, P2.

12th row As 2nd row.

13th–16th rows As 1st and 2nd rows.

These 16 rows form *panel F* and are rep as required.

PANEL G

Worked over 23 sts.

1st row (rs facing) P2, K1 tbl, P6, Cr2B, P6, K1 tbl, P2.

2nd row K2, P1, K6, P5, K6, P1, K2.

3rd row P2, K1 tbl, P5, BCr, K1, FCrP, P5, K1 tbl, P2.

4th row and every foll ws row K all K sts and P all P sts.

5th row P2, K1 tbl, P4, BCr, P1, K1, P1, FCrP, P4, K1 tbl, P2.

7th row P2, K1 tbl, P3, BCr, (K1, P1) twice, K1, FCrP, P3, K1 tbl, P2.

9th row P2, K1 tbl, P2, BCr, (K1, P1) 3 times, K1, FCrP, P2, K1 tbl, P2.

11th row P2, K1 tbl, P1, BCr, (K1, P1) 4 times, K1, FCrP, P1, K1 tbl, P2.

13th row P2, K1 tbl, P1, K2, P3, K2, P1, K2, P3, K2, P1, K1 tbl, P2.

14th row As 4th row.

These 14 rows form *panel G* and are rep as required.

BACK

With 3¾mm (US 4) needles cast on 123(131) sts and work in twisted cable rib as foll:

1st row (rs facing) K3, *(P1, K1 tbl) twice, P1, K3, rep from * to end.

2nd row and every foll ws row P3, *(K1, P1 tbl) twice, K1, P3, rep from * to end.

3rd row K3, *P1, sl next 2 sts onto CN and hold at front of work, K1 tbl, then P1, K1 tbl from CN, P1, K3, rep from * to end.

5th and 7th rows As 1st row.

8th row As 2nd row.

Rep these 8 rows 3 times more, but on last row inc 14(18) sts evenly across row. (137(149) sts – 32 rib rows worked.)

Change to 4mm (US 5) needles and place patt panels as foll:

1st row (rs facing) Work *1st rows of panels* as foll: 7(13) sts of panel A, then panels B, C, D, E, D, F, G, F, D, E, D, C, B, and finally 7(13) sts of panel A.

2nd row Work *2nd rows of panels* as

foll: 7(13) sts of panel A, then panels B, C, D, E, D, F, G, F, D, E, D, C, B, and finally 7(13) sts of panel A.

The panels are now set. Cont to rep the various patt rows of each panel as required until back measures 62(65)cm (24½(25½)in) from cast-on edge, ending with a ws row.

Shape back neck

Next row Patt 56(62), turn and work on this first set of sts only.
**Keeping patts correct, cast off 5 sts at beg (neck edge) on next row and foll 2 alt rows. Cast off rem 41(47) sts.

With rs facing rejoin yarn to rem sts, cast off centre 25 sts and patt to end of row. Patt 1 row.
Now work as for first side from ** to end.

FRONT

Work as for back until front measures 40(43)cm (15¾(17)in) from cast-on edge, ending with a ws row.

Shape front neck

Next row Patt 68(74), turn and work on this first set of sts only.
***Keeping patts correct, dec 1 st

at neck edge on next row and every foll alt row until 41(47) sts rem.
Now cont straight until front measures same as back to cast-off shoulder edge ending at side edge. Cast off.
Return to rem sts and sl centre st onto a safety pin, with rs facing rejoin yarn to rem sts and patt to end of row.
Now work as for first side from *** to end.

SLEEVES

With 3¾mm (US 4) needles cast on 51 sts and work in twisted cable rib as for back welt for 24 rows, but inc 22 sts evenly across last row. (73 sts)
Change to 4mm (US 5) needles and place patt panels as foll:
1st row (rs facing) Work *1st rows of panels* as foll: 5 sts of panel A, then panels, D, F, G, F, D, and finally 5 sts of panel A.
2nd row Work *2nd rows of panels* as foll: 5 sts of panel A, then panels D, F, G, F, D, and finally 5 sts of panel A.

Cont to rep the various patt rows of each panel as required, *at the same time*, inc 1 st at both ends of every foll 3rd row, working inc sts into moss st at either side, until there are 131(133) sts on the needle.
Now cont straight until sleeve measures 43(45)cm (17(17¾)in) from cast-on edge, ending with a ws row.
Cast off fairly loosely.
Rep patt for second sleeve.

NECKBAND

Join right shoulder seam.
With the 3¾mm (US 4) circular needle and rs facing, pick up and K 59 sts down left front neck, K centre front st, pick up and K 59 sts up right front neck and finally 55 sts from back neck. (174 sts)
Work in *rows* of twisted cable rib and single rib as foll:
1st row (ws facing) K1, (P1, K1) 27 times, P3, *K1, (P1 tbl, K1) twice, P3, rep from * to within 2 sts of centre st, P2 tog, P1, P2 tog tbl, P1, ** (K1, P1 tbl) twice, K1, P3, rep from ** to end.
2nd row Work as for 1st row of rib on back welt to within 2 sts of centre st, K2 tog tbl, K1, K2 tog, patt next 57 sts as for 1st row of rib on back welt, work across back in K1, P1 rib as set.
Work in ribs as now set, back neck in K1, P1, rib and front neck in twisted cabled rib, and keeping continuity of centre 5 sts, cont in ribs for 15 rows, dec as set on every row.
Cast off evenly in patt as set, dec as set.

TO MAKE UP

Join left shoulder and neckband seam. With centre of cast-off edges of sleeves to shoulder seams, sew sleeves carefully in position, reaching down to same depth on front and back. Join side and sleeve seams.

CLASSIC FAIR ISLE CARDIGAN

This children's cardigan has the same pattern as the 1930's Fair Isle on page 85 but the change of colourway and style make it look entirely different. It is a very versatile garment for boys and girls, and the cotton yarn washes well and retains its shape. With its subtle colours that never date, this would make an ideal present.

MEASUREMENTS

To fit approx age 2–3 (4:6:7–8) years.
Actual measurement 55(60:64:70)cm (21¾(23¾:25¼:27½)in).
Full length 30(36:38:41)cm (11¾(14¼:15:16¼)in).
Sleeve seam (cuff turned down) approx 23(26:30:32)cm (9(10¼:11¾:12½)in).

MATERIALS

Rowan Cabled Mercerised Cotton 50g balls.
Main colour (MC) cream (301) 3(3:4:4) balls;
1st contrast colour (A) black (319) 1 ball;
2nd contrast colour (B) navy (330) 1 ball;
3rd contrast colour (C) granit (325) 1 ball;
4th contrast colour (D) souris (318) 1 ball;
5th contrast colour (E) olive (327) 1 ball;
6th contrast colour (F) yellow (305) 1 ball.
Equivalent yarn: 3-ply.
1 pair each of 2¼mm (US 0) and 3mm (US 2) knitting needles.
One 2¼mm (US 0) and one 3mm (US 2) circular needle.
7(7:8:8) buttons.
2 safety pins.
2 spare needles.

TENSION

34 sts and 37 rows to 10cm (4in) on 3mm (US 2) needles over Fair Isle patt. See page 10.

BODY

Worked in one piece.
With the 2¼mm (US 0) circular needle and MC, cast on 199(215:229:249) sts and work in single rib in *rows* as foll:
1st row (rs facing) K1, *P1, K1, rep from * to end.
2nd row P1, *K1, P1, rep from * to end.

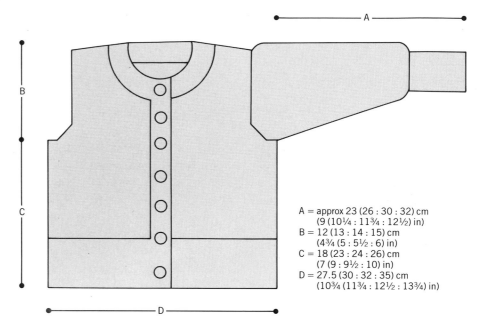

A = approx 23 (26 : 30 : 32) cm (9 (10¼ : 11¾ : 12½) in)
B = 12 (13 : 14 : 15) cm (4¾ (5 : 5½ : 6) in)
C = 18 (23 : 24 : 26) cm (7 (9 : 9½ : 10) in)
D = 27.5 (30 : 32 : 35) cm (10¾ (11¾ : 12½ : 13¾) in)

Rep last 2 rows until 4 rows have been worked in all.
Buttonhole row (rs facing) Rib 4, cast off 3 sts, rib to end.
Next row Rib, casting on 3 sts over cast-off sts on previous row. Rib a further 14 rows, and then work the 2 buttonhole rows again. Cont in rib until welt measures 6cm (2½in), ending with a rs row.
Next row Rib 11 sts, and transfer these sts to a safety pin for left front border, rib to end of row and slip last 11 sts onto second safety pin for right front border, and cont on middle set of 177(193:207:227) sts only. Change to the 3mm (US 2) circular needle and cont in *rows* as foll:
Inc row K and inc 4 sts evenly across row. (181(197:211:231) sts)
Next row P.
Now starting with a K row work in st st from chart as foll:
1st row (rs facing) Work 0(8:5:5) sts before the dotted line, rep the 20 st patt to last 1(9:6:6) st(s), work 1(9:6:6) st(s) beyond the dotted line.
2nd row Work 1(9:6:6) st(s) before the dotted line, rep the 20 st patt to last 0(8:5:5) sts, work 0(8:5:5) sts beyond the dotted line.

Cont straight foll chart, rep the 30 rows as required until work measures 18(23:24:26)cm (7(9:9½:10¼)in) from cast-on edge, ending with a ws row.
Divide for fronts and back
Next row Patt across 40(45:47:54) sts, cast off next 8(8:10:10) sts, patt 85(91:97:103) sts, cast off 8(8:10:10) sts, patt rem 40(45:47:54) sts. Work on middle set of 85(91:97:103) sts only leaving sts for right and left fronts on spare needles.
Back
With ws facing and using the straight 3mm (US 2) needles, rejoin yarn to the 85(91:97:103) sts of back.
Shape armholes
Keeping patt correct, dec 1 st at both ends of next 4 rows. (77(83:89:95)sts)
Now cont straight until back measures 30(36:38:41)cm (11¾(14¼:15:16¼)in) from cast-on edge, ending with a ws row.
Shape shoulders
Keeping patt correct, cast off 10(11:12:13) sts at beg of next 4 rows.
Leave rem 37(39:41:43) sts on a spare needle.

Right front

With ws facing and using the straight 3mm (US 2) needles, rejoin yarn to the 40(45:47:54) sts of right front.

Shape armhole

Keeping patt correct, dec 1 st at armhole edge on next 4 rows. (36(41:43:50) sts)

Now cont straight until front measures 26(31:33:35)cm (10¼(12¼:13:13¾)in) from cast-on edge, ending at centre front edge.

Shape front neck

Keeping patt correct cast off 6(7:7:8) sts at beg (neck edge) on next row, 3(4:3:4) sts on foll 2 alt rows, and then 1 st on next 4(4:6:8) rows. (20(22:24:26) sts)

Now cont straight until front measures same as back to beg of shoulder shaping, ending at armhole edge.

Shape shoulder

Keeping patt correct, cast off 10(11:12:13) sts at beg of next row and foll alt row.

Left front

With ws facing and using the straight 3mm (US 2) needles, rejoin yarn to the 40(45:47:54) sts of left front and work as for right front reversing shapings.

SLEEVES

With 2¼mm (US 0) needles and MC cast on 45(49:51:55) sts and work in single rib as for body welt for 7cm (2¾in) ending with a 2nd row.

Change to 3mm (US 2) needles.

Inc row K and inc 18 sts evenly across row. (63(67:69:73) sts)

Next row P.

Now starting with a K row work in st st from chart, starting on 15th(23rd:11th:13th) row as foll:

15th(23rd:11th:13th) row (rs facing) Work 1(3:4:6) st(s) before the dotted line, rep the 20 st patt to last 2(4:5:7) sts, work 2(4:5:7) sts beyond the dotted line.

The chart is now placed. Cont straight foll chart, rep the 30 rows as required until sleeve measures approx 23(26:30:32)cm (9(10¼:11¾:12½)in) from cast-on edge, ending with a ws row and on same patt row as back/front to beg of armhole shaping.

Shape top

Cast off 4(4:5:5) sts at beg of next 2 rows.

Keeping patt correct, dec 1 st at each end of every foll alt row until 29 sts rem. Now dec 1 st at each end of every row until 11 sts rem.

Next row K1, (K2 tog) along row.

Cast off rem 6 sts.

Rep patt for second sleeve.

TO MAKE UP

Join both shoulder seams. Sew sleeve seams matching patts. Set sleeves into armholes gathering any fullness evenly across top of shoulder.

BUTTON BAND

With 2¼mm (US 0) needles and MC rejoin yarn to sts on safety pin at left front and cont in rib as set until band, when slightly stretched, fits up left front to beg of neck shaping, sewing in position as you go along. Leave sts on safety pin.

On this band mark positions for 6(6:7:7) buttons. First 2 buttons already placed by buttonholes in welt, last button to come 3cm (1¼in) down from neck edge and rem buttons spaced evenly between.

BUTTONHOLE BAND

Work as for button band with the addition of buttonholes, worked as before, when button positions are reached. Leave sts on safety pin.

NECKBAND

With 2¼mm (US 0) needles and MC and rs facing, rib across sts of right front band, pick up and K 33(35:35:37) sts up right front neck, K across centre back sts, pick up and K 33(35:35:37) sts down left front neck and finally rib across sts of left front band. (125(131:133:139) sts)

Keeping rib as set for bands, work in single rib for 1 row. Now work a buttonhole on next 2 rows.

Rib 4 more rows.

Cast off loosely ribwise.

Sew on buttons to correspond with buttonholes and turn cuffs up to required depth.

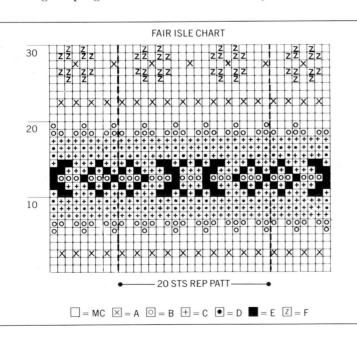

FAIR ISLE CHART

◀——— 20 STS REP PATT ———▶

☐ = MC ☒ = A ⊙ = B ⊞ = C ⦿ = D ■ = E ☒ = F

RUSSIAN
FITTED CARDIGAN

The shape of this cardigan was inspired by the Cossack jackets of Imperialist Russia, and the idea for the pattern came from an antique paisley shawl. Its fitted shape is particularly flattering and sparkling buttons can dress it up for evening wear. The silk and wool in which this garment is knitted lend themselves best to vivid colours, so an alternative colourway might be purple, red, fuchsia and bright blue on a black background.

MEASUREMENTS

One size only to fit bust
81–91cm (32–36in).
Actual measurement
102cm (40in).
Full length 62cm (24½in).
Sleeve seam 42cm (16½in).

MATERIALS

Rowan Silk and Wool 25g balls.
Main colour (MC) red (842)
18 balls;
1st contrast colour (A) purple
(841) 1 ball;
2nd contrast colour (B) emerald
(850) 1 ball;
3rd contrast colour (C) fuchsia
(843) 1 ball;
4th contrast colour (D) gold (847)
1 ball.
Equivalent yarn: 4-ply.
1 pair each of 2¼mm (US 0),
3mm (US 2) and 3¼mm (US 3)
knitting needles.
15 buttons.

TENSION

28 sts and 36 rows to 10cm (4in)
on 3¼mm (US 3) needles over
st st. See page 10.

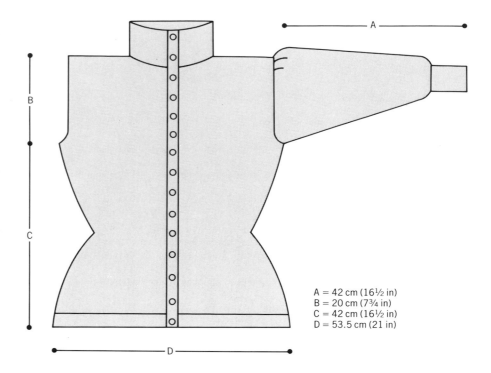

A = 42 cm (16½ in)
B = 20 cm (7¾ in)
C = 42 cm (16½ in)
D = 53.5 cm (21 in)

SPECIAL ABBREVIATION

M1 = make 1 st by picking up
loop that lies between st just
worked and foll st and working
into back of it.

RIGHT FRONT

With 3mm (US 2) needles and
MC cast on 75 sts and work in

single rib as foll:
1st row (rs facing) K1, *P1, K1,
rep from * to end.
2nd row P1, *K1, P1, rep from *
to end.
Rep these 2 rows for 3cm (1¼in)
ending with a 2nd row.
Change to 3¼mm (US 3) needles
and starting with a K row work in

RIGHT FRONT CHART

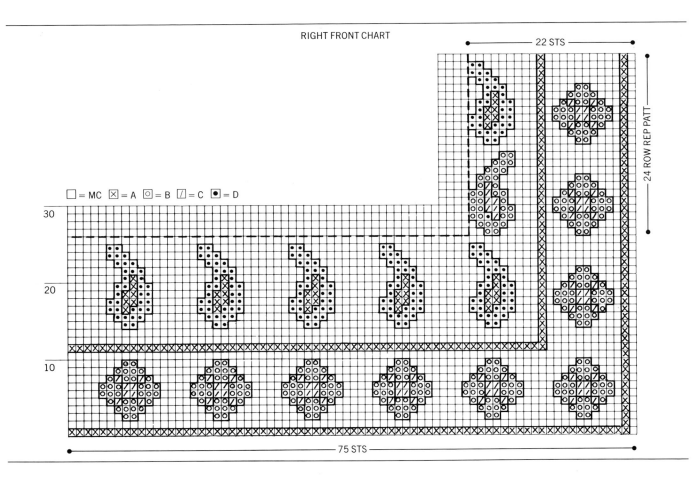

□ = MC ☒ = A ◉ = B ⧄ = C ● = D

st st from *right front chart*, working in patt as shown until 26th row has been worked. Now cont foll chart working the 22 sts at front edge in patt and rem sts in MC only, and rep the 24 rows as indicated up right front, *at the same time* shape as foll:

1st dec row (rs facing – 27th row of chart) Patt 22 sts from chart, K4, K2 tog, *K6, K2 tog, K2, K2 tog, rep from * to last 11 sts, K6, K2 tog, K3. (67 sts)
Cont straight in patt as set for 11 rows.

2nd dec row (rs facing) Patt 22 sts from chart, K4, K2 tog, *K4, K2 tog, K2, K2 tog, rep from * to last 9 sts, K4, K2 tog, K3. (59 sts)
Cont straight in patt as set for 11 rows.

3rd dec row (rs facing) Patt 22 sts from chart, K4, *K2 tog, K2, rep from * to last st, K1. (51 sts)
Cont straight in patt as set for 23 rows.

1st inc row (rs facing) Patt 22 sts from chart, K4, *M1, K3, rep from * to last st, K1. (59 sts)
Cont straight in patt as set for 23 rows.

2nd inc row (rs facing) Patt 22 sts from chart, K5, M1, *K5, M1, K3, M1, rep from * to last 8 sts, K5, M1, K3. (67 sts)
Cont in patt as set, *at the same time*, inc 1 st at side edge (edge in MC) on every foll 6th row until there are 71 sts on the needle.
Now cont straight keeping centre front patt correct, until front measures 42cm (16½in) from cast-on edge ending at side edge.

Shape armhole
Cast off 9 sts at beg of next row.
Now dec 1 st at armhole edge on next row and every foll alt row until 54 sts rem.
Now cont straight until 170 patt rows in all have been worked (14 little roses complete and paisley in D complete).

Now starting with the 171st row, which is a K row, work from *right front neck chart* on 36 sts nearest to front edge, noting that no more paisleys are to be worked and all rem sts to be worked in MC. Cont foll chart until 194th row has been worked.

Shape front neck
(rs facing) Cast off 14 sts at beg of next row.
Keeping chart correct, dec 1 st at neck edge on next 8 rows. (32 sts)
Now cont straight until the 211 rows of chart are complete.
Cast off.

LEFT FRONT
With 3mm (US 2) needles and MC cast on 75 sts and work in single rib as foll:
1st row (rs facing) K1, *P1, K1, rep from * to end.
2nd row P1, *K1, P1, rep from * to end.
Rep these 2 rows for 3cm (1¼in)

ending with a 1st row.

Change to 3¼mm (US 3) needles and starting with a P row (ws row), work in st st from *right front chart* (this reverses chart and front).

Work as for right front, working odd numbered rows as P rows (reading from right to left) and even numbered rows as K rows (reading from left to right) also reverse all shapings by working first dec row on 28th row and working all foll dec and inc rows with WS facing.

When 170 patt rows in all have been worked cont to work from right front neck chart, noting that 171st row is a P row.

BACK

With 3mm (US 2) needles and MC cast on 150 sts and work in K1, P1, rib for 3cm (1¼in). Change to 3¼mm (US 3) needles and starting with a K row work in st st from *back chart* as foll:
1st row (rs facing) Work 3 sts before the dotted line, rep the 12 st patt 12 times, work 3 sts beyond the dotted line.
Cont as now set until 26 rows of chart have been worked. Now cont in MC only and shape as foll:
1st dec row (rs facing) (K6, K2

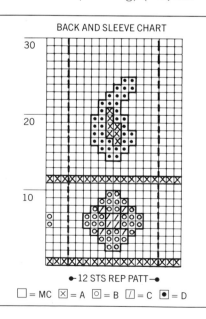

BACK AND SLEEVE CHART

◆─12 STS REP PATT─◆

□ = MC ⊠ = A ◎ = B ⧄ = C ● = D

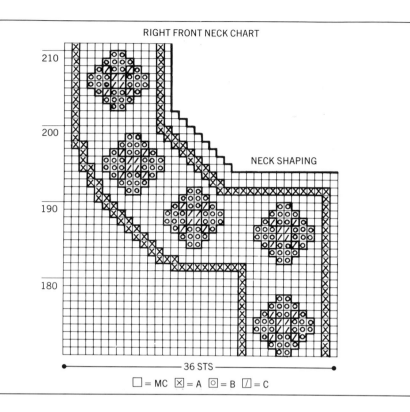

RIGHT FRONT NECK CHART

NECK SHAPING

◆────── 36 STS ──────◆

□ = MC ⊠ = A ◎ = B ⧄ = C

tog) 8 times, K22, (K2 tog, K6) 8 times. (134 sts)
Cont straight in st st for 11 rows.
2nd dec row (rs facing) (K6, K2 tog, K4, K2 tog) 4 times, K22, (K2 tog, K4, K2 tog, K6) 4 times. (118 sts)
Cont straight in st st for 11 rows.
3rd dec row (rs facing) (K4, K2 tog) 8 times, K22, (K2 tog, K4) 8 times. (102 sts)
Cont straight in st st for 23 rows.
1st inc row (rs facing) (K5, M1) 8 times, K22, (M1, K5) 8 times. (118 sts)
Cont straight in st st for 23 rows.
2nd inc row (K7, M1, K5, M1) 4 times, K22, (M1, K5, M1, K7) 4 times. (134 sts)
Cont in st st, *at the same time*, inc 1 st at each end of every foll 6th row until there are 142 sts on the needle.
Now cont straight until back measures 42cm (16½in) from cast-on edge, ending with a ws row.
Shape armholes
Cast off 9 sts at beg of next 2 rows. Dec 1 st at each end of next row

and every foll alt row until 106 sts rem.
Now cont straight until 190 rows in all have been worked from top of rib, thus ending with a ws row. Now place *back neck border chart* as foll:
191st row K30MC, now work across the 46 sts of chart, K30MC.
Cont to foll chart working over centre sts as set and rem sts in MC until 203rd row of chart has been worked, thus ending with a rs row.
Shape back neck
Next row Patt 39 sts, cast off centre 28 sts, patt to end of row and cont on this last set of 39 sts only.
**Keeping patt correct, dec 1 st at neck edge on next 7 rows. Cast off rem 32 sts.
With rs facing rejoin yarn to rem sts and work as for first side from ** to end.

SLEEVES

With 2¼mm (US 0) needles and MC, cast on 58 sts and work in K1, P1, rib for 8cm (3in).

Inc row Rib and inc 20 sts evenly across row. (78 sts)
Change to 3¼mm (US 3) needles and starting with a K row work in st st from *sleeves chart* as foll:
1st row (rs facing) Work 3 sts before the dotted line, rep the 12 st patt 6 times, work 3 sts beyond the dotted line.
The chart is now set. Cont to foll chart until the 26 rows have been worked. Now cont in MC only.
Inc row (rs facing) K2, M1, K12, M1, K to last 14 sts, M1, K12, M1, K2.
Cont in st st and work the inc row as set on every foll 8th row working incs in same positions as previous incs, until there are 122 sts on the needle.
Now cont straight until sleeve measures 42cm (16½in) from cast-on edge, ending with a ws row.
Shape top
Cast off 5 sts at beg of next 2 rows.
Now dec 1 st at both ends of next row and every foll alt row until 64 sts rem.
Now dec 1 st at both ends of every row until 34 sts rem.
Cast off.
Rep patt for second sleeve.

BUTTON BAND
With 3mm (US 2) needles and MC and rs facing, pick up and K

164 sts evenly down left front edge.
Work in K1, P1, rib for 8 rows.
Cast off loosely ribwise.

BUTTONHOLE BAND
With 3mm (US 2) needles and MC and rs facing, pick up and K 164 sts evenly up right front edge.
Work in P1, K1, rib for 3 rows.
Buttonhole row (rs facing) Rib 4, *cast off 2 sts, rib 11, rep from * to last 4 sts, cast off 2 sts, rib to end.
Next row Rib, casting on 2 sts over cast-off sts on previous row. (13 buttonholes worked.)
Rib 3 more rows.
Cast off loosely ribwise.

COLLAR
Join both shoulder seams matching patts.
With 3mm (US 2) needles and MC and rs facing, pick up and K 36 sts from top of buttonhole band and around to right shoulder, 44 sts across back neck, and 36 sts around left front neck and button band. (116 sts)
Work in K1, P1, rib for 7 rows.
Next row (rs facing) Rib 4, cast off 2 sts, rib to end.
Next row Rib, casting on 2 sts over cast-off sts on previous row.
Work a further 10 rows in rib, then work the 2 buttonhole

rows once more.
Work 20 rows in rib, then work the 2 buttonhole rows once more.
Work 10 rows in rib, then work the 2 buttonhole rows once more.
Work 8 rows in rib.
Cast off loosely ribwise.

TO MAKE UP
Fold collar in half to inside and carefully sl st in position, sewing around buttonholes and catching together front edges. Join side and sleeve seams. Set sleeves into armholes gathering fullness evenly across top of shoulders. Sew on buttons to correspond with buttonholes.

BACK NECK CHART

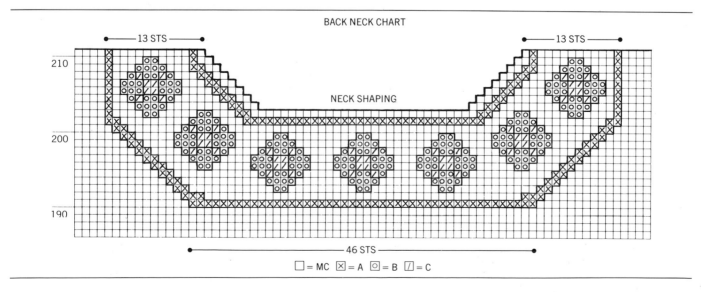

13 STS   13 STS

210

NECK SHAPING

200

190

46 STS

□ = MC ☒ = A ⊙ = B ⧄ = C

SUMMER COTTON SWEATERS

The Long Cable-stitch Sweater on the left in the photograph is a popular 1920's style which looks good with a long lean skirt. The High-necked Aran, modelled by the man, is my husband Dick's favourite sweater. It works equally well in navy or black and looks good on all the men I know. The Fisherman's Aran is a familiar style for men, with its rows of bobbles, and women have been known to steal them, as in the photograph. The pattern for this sweater is featured on page 52. Also part of this collection is the Tree Bobble Sweater for girls. It gets its name from the clusters of bobbles with stems which look like little trees.

LONG CABLE-STITCH SWEATER

MEASUREMENTS
To fit bust 86–91(97:102)cm
(34–36(38:40)in).
Actual measurement
106(112:118)cm
(41¾(44:46½)in).
Full length 72(75:78)cm
(28¼(29½:30¾)in).
Sleeve seam 47cm (18½in).

MATERIALS
Rowan Cabled Mercerised Cotton
50g balls.
Cream (301) 14(14:15) balls.
Equivalent yarn: 3-ply.
1 pair each of 2¼mm (US 0) and
3mm (US 2) knitting needles.
Cable needle.
4 spare needles.

TENSION
30 sts and 38 rows to 10cm (4in)
on 3mm (US 2) needles over st st.
See page 10.

SPECIAL ABBREVIATIONS
C2F = slip next 2 sts onto CN and
leave at front of work, K next 2
sts, then K the 2 sts from CN.
C2B = slip next 2 sts onto CN and
leave at back of work, K next 2
sts, then K the 2 sts from CN.

CABLE PANEL
Worked over 13 sts.
1st row (rs facing) P2, K9, P2.
2nd row K2, P9, K2.
3rd row P2, C2F, K1, C2B, P2.
4th row As 2nd row.
Rep 1st and 2nd rows once more.
These 6 rows form the *cable panel*
and are rep as required.

MOSS STITCH PANEL
Worked over 15 sts.
1st row (rs facing) K15.
2nd row P15.
3rd row K7, P1, K7.

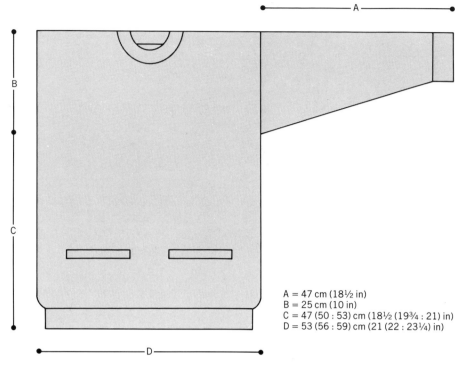

A = 47 cm (18½ in)
B = 25 cm (10 in)
C = 47 (50 : 53) cm (18½ (19¾ : 21) in)
D = 53 (56 : 59) cm (21 (22 : 23¼) in)

4th row P6, K1, P1, K1, P6.
5th row K5, (P1, K1) twice, P1, K5.
6th row P4, (K1, P1) 3 times, K1, P4.
7th row K3, (P1, K1) 4 times, P1, K3.
8th row P2, (K1, P1) 5 times, K1, P2.
9th row K1, P13, K1.
10th row P2, K11, P2.
11th row As 1st row.
12th row As 2nd row.
13th row As 1st row.
14th row As 10th row.
15th–23rd rows As 9th–1st rows (working in reverse order).
24th row As 2nd row.
25th–30th rows Rep 1st and 2nd rows 3 times more.
These 30 rows form the *moss stitch panel* and are rep as required.

BACK
With 2¼mm (US 0) needles cast on 156(164:172) sts and work in K2, P2, rib for 5cm (2in).
Inc row Rib and inc 23 sts evenly across row. (179(187:195)sts)
Change to 3mm (US 2) needles and place patt as foll:

1st row (rs facing) K13(17:21), *work across 1st row of *cable panel*, work across 1st row of *moss stitch panel*, rep from * to last 26(30:34) sts, work across 1st row of *cable panel*, K13(17:21).
2nd row P13(17:21), *work across 2nd row of *cable panel*, work across 2nd row of *moss stitch panel*, rep from * to last 26(30:34) sts, work across 2nd row of *cable panel*, P13(17:21).
Cont in patts as now set, rep the 6 rows and 30 rows as required, and keeping side edges in st st until back measures 67(70:73)cm (26½(27½:28½)in) from cast-on edge, ending with a ws row.
Shape back neck
Next row Patt 68(71:74), turn, work 2 tog, patt to end and work on this last set of 67(70:73) sts only.
**Keeping patt correct, dec 1 st at neck edge on every row until 63(66:69) sts rem.
Now work a few rows straight until back measures 72(75:78)cm (28¼(29½:30¾)in) from cast-on edge, ending with a ws row.
Cast off.

Return to rem sts and sl centre 43(45:47) sts onto a spare needle, with rs facing rejoin yarn to rem 68(71:74) sts and patt to end of row.

Next row Patt to last 2 sts, work 2 tog.

Now work as for first side from ** to end.

POCKET LININGS

With 3mm (US 2) needles cast on 45 sts and starting with a K row work in st st for 12cm (4¾in), ending with a ws row.

Leave sts on a spare needle.

Rep patt for second pocket lining.

FRONT

Work as for back until front measures 17cm (6¾in) from cast-on edge, ending with a ws row.

Place pockets

Next row Patt 25(29:33), *slip next 45 sts on a spare needle and in their place patt across the 45 sts from first pocket lining*, patt next 39 sts, now work from * to * once more but working across sts of second pocket lining, patt to end. Now cont in patt across the 179(187:195) sts until front measures 65(68:71)cm (25½(26¾:28)in) from cast-on edge, ending with a ws row.

Shape front neck

Next row Patt 71(74:77), turn, work 2 tog, patt to end and work on this last set of 70(73:76) sts only.

***Keeping patt correct, dec 1 st at neck edge on every row until 63(66:69) sts rem.

Now cont straight until front measures same as back to cast-off shoulder edge, ending on same patt row.

Cast off.

Return to rem sts and sl centre 37(39:41) sts onto a spare needle, with rs facing rejoin yarn to rem 71(74:77) sts and patt to end of row.

Next row Patt to last 2 sts, work 2 tog.

Now work as for first side from *** to end.

SLEEVES

With 2¼mm (US 0) needles cast on 68 sts and work in K2, P2, rib for 5cm (2in).

Inc row Rib and inc 27 sts evenly across row. (95 sts)

Change to 3mm (US 2) needles and place patt as foll:

1st row (rs facing) K13, *work across 1st row of *cable panel*, work across 1st row of *moss stitch panel*, rep from * once more, work across 1st row of *cable panel*, K13.

Cont in patts as now set, keeping side edges in st st, *at the same time*, inc 1 st at both ends of every foll 4th row until there are 161 sts on the needle, working inc sts into st st at either side.

Now cont straight until sleeve measures 47cm (18½in) from cast-on edge, ending with a ws row.

Cast off fairly loosely.
Rep patt for second sleeve.

NECKBAND

Join right shoulder seam carefully matching patts.
With 2¼mm (US 0) needles and rs facing, pick up and K 34 sts down left front neck, K across centre front sts, pick up and K 34 sts up right front neck, 20 sts down right back neck, K across centre back sts and finally pick up and K 20 sts up left back neck. (188(192:196) sts)
Work in K2, P2, rib for 12 rows.
Cast off loosely ribwise.

POCKET TOPS

With 2¼mm (US 0) needles and rs facing, work in K2, P2, rib across the 45 sts held on one spare needle, dec 1 st on 1st row. (44 sts)
Cont in rib as set for 7 rows.
Cast off fairly loosely ribwise.

TO MAKE UP

Join left shoulder and neckband seam. Fold neckband in half to inside and sl st loosely in position. With centre of cast-off edges of sleeves to shoulder seams, sew

sleeves carefully in position reaching down to same depth on front and back. Join side and sleeve seams. Catch down side edges of pocket tops and sl st pocket linings neatly in position on wrong side.

HIGH-NECKED ARAN FOR MEN

MEASUREMENTS

To fit chest
86–91(97–102:107–112)cm
(34–36(38–40:42–44)in).
Actual measurement
104(116:128)cm
(41(45¾:50¼)in).
Full length 65(68:70)cm
(25½(26¾:27½)in).
Sleeve seam (with cuff turned down) 50cm (19¾in).

MATERIALS

Rowan Handknit D.K. Cotton 50g balls.
Ecru (251) 24(24:25) balls.
Equivalent yarn: D.K.
1 pair each of 3¾mm (US 4) and 4mm (US 5) knitting needles.
Cable needle.

TENSION

20 sts and 28 rows to 10cm (4in) on 4mm (US 5) needles over st st. See page 10.

SPECIAL ABBREVIATIONS

C2F = sl next 2 sts onto CN and leave at front of work, K next 2 sts, then K the 2 sts from CN.
BCr = sl next st onto CN and leave at back of work, K next 2 sts, then P the st from CN.
FCr = sl next 2 sts onto CN and leave at front of work, K next st, then K the 2 sts from CN.
FCrP = sl next 2 sts onto CN and leave at front of work, P next st, then K the 2 sts from CN.
M1 = pick up horizontal loop that

lies between st just worked and foll st, and work into back of it.

PANEL A

Worked over a multiple of 2 sts plus 1.
1st row (rs facing) P1, *K1, P1, rep from * to end.
2nd row P1, *K1, P1, rep from * to end.
These 2 rows from *panel A* and are rep as required.

PANEL B

Worked over 8 sts.
1st row (rs facing) K1B, P1, K4, P1, K1B.
2nd row and every foll ws row P1, K1, P4, K1, P1.
3rd row K1B, P1, C2F, P1, K1B.
5th and 7th rows As 1st row.
8th row As 2nd row.
These 8 rows form *panel B* and are rep as required.

PANEL C

Worked over 11 sts.
1st row (rs facing) P1, K9, P1.
2nd row K1, P9, K1.
3rd row P11.
4th row K1, P9, K1.
These 4 rows form *panel C* and are rep as required.

PANEL D

Worked over 15 sts.
1st row (rs facing) P1, K1, P1, K12.
2nd row P11, (K1, P1) twice.
3rd row K2, P1, K1, P1, K10.
4th row P9, K1, P1, K1, P3.
5th row K4, P1, K1, P1, K8.
6th row P7, K1, P1, K1, P5.
7th row K6, P1, K1, P1, K6.
8th row P5, K1, P1, K1, P7.
9th row K8, P1, K1, P1, K4.
10th row P3, K1, P1, K1, P9.
11th row K10, P1, K1, P1, K2.
12th row (P1, K1) twice, P11.
13th row K12, P1, K1, P1.
14th row As 12th row.
15th–24th rows Work 11th–2nd rows in reverse order.

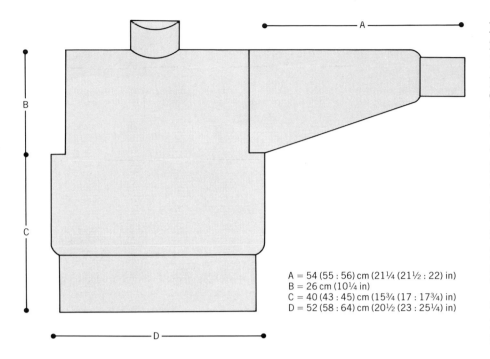

A = 54 (55 : 56) cm (21¼ (21½ : 22) in)
B = 26 cm (10¼ in)
C = 40 (43 : 45) cm (15¾ (17 : 17¾) in)
D = 52 (58 : 64) cm (20½ (23 : 25¼) in)

These 24 rows form *panel D* and are rep as required.

PANEL E
Worked over 30 sts.
1st row (rs facing) P6, C2F, P10, C2F, P6.
2nd row and every foll ws row K all K sts and P all P sts.
3rd row P5, BCr, FCr, P8, BCr, FCr, P5.
5th row P4, BCr, K1, P1, FCr, P6, BCr, K1, P1, FCr, P4.
7th row P3, BCr, (K1, P1) twice, FCr, P4, BCr, (K1, P1) twice, FCr, P3.
9th row P2, *BCr, (K1, P1) 3 times, FCr, P2, rep from * once.
11th row P1, *BCr, (K1, P1) 4 times, FCr, rep from * once, P1.
13th row P1, K2, (K1, P1) 5 times, C2F, (K1, P1) 5 times, K2, P1.
15th row P1, *FCrP, (K1, P1) 4 times, BCr, rep from * once, P1.
17th row P2, *FCrP, (K1, P1) 3 times, BCr, P2, rep from * once.
19th row P3, FCrP, (K1, P1) twice, BCr, P4, FCrP, (K1, P1) twice, BCr, P3.
21st row P4, FCrP, K1, P1, BCr, P6, FcrP, K1, P1, BCr, P4.

23rd row P5, FCrP, BCr, P8, FCrP, BCr, P5.
24th row As 2nd row.
These 24 rows form *panel E* and are rep as required.

BACK
With 3¾mm (US 4) needles cast on 123(135:147) sts and work in cabled rib as foll:
1st row (rs facing) P1, (K1, P1) 4(7:10) times, K4, *P1, (K1, P1) 3 times, K4*, rep from * to * 4 times, P1, (K1, P1) 4 times, K4, now rep from * to * 4 times, P1, (K1, P1) 4(7:10) times.
2nd row and every foll ws row K1, (P1, K1) 4(7:10) times, P4, *K1, (P1, K1) 3 times, P4*, rep from * to * 4 times, K1, (P1, K1) 4 times, P4, now rep from * to * 4 times, K1, (P1, K1) 4(7:10) times.
3rd row P1, (K1, P1) 4(7:10) times, C2F, *P1, (K1, P1) 3 times, C2F*, rep from * to * 4 times, P1, (K1, P1) 4 times, C2F, now rep from * to * 4 times, P1, (K1, P1) 4(7:10) times.
5th and 7th rows As 1st row.
8th row As 2nd row.
Rep these 8 rows until 39 rows of rib have been worked.

Inc row (ws facing) Patt 22(28:34), M1, patt 27, M1, patt 13, M1, patt 12, M1, patt 27, M1, patt 22(28:34). (128(140:152) sts)
Change to 4mm (US 5) needles and place patt panels as foll:
1st row (rs facing) Work *1st rows of panels* as foll: 7(13:19) sts of panel A, then panels B, C, D, B, E, B, D, C, B, and finally 7(13:19) sts of panel A.
2nd row Work *2nd rows of panels* as foll: 7(13:19) sts of panel A, then panels B, C, D, B, E, B, D, C, B, and finally 7(13:19) sts of panel A. The panels are now set. Cont to rep the various patt rows of each panel as required until back measures 40(43:45)cm (15¾(17:17¾)in) from cast-on edge, ending with a ws row.
Shape armholes
Cast off 8(10:12) sts at beg of next 2 rows. (112(120:128) sts)
Now keeping patts correct, cont straight until back measures 65(68:70)cm (25½(26¾:27½)in) from cast-on edge, ending with a ws row.
Shape shoulders
Cast off 34(37:40) sts at beg of next 2 rows.
Cast off rem 44(46:48) sts.

FRONT
Work as for back until front measures 60(63:65)cm (23½(24¾:25½)in) from cast-on edge, ending with a ws row.
Shape front neck
Next row Patt 46(47:49), turn and work on this first set of sts only.
**Keeping patts correct, cast off 2 sts at beg (neck edge) on next row and foll 2 alt rows. Now dec 1 st at neck edge on every row until 34(37:40) sts rem.
Work a few rows straight in patt until front measures same as back to cast-off shoulder edge, ending at armhole edge. Cast off.
With rs facing rejoin yarn to rem sts, cast off centre 20(26:30) sts,

patt to end of row. Work 1 row.
Now work as for first side from **
to end.

SLEEVES

With 3¾mm (US 4) needles cast
on 57 sts and work in cabled rib as
foll:

1st row *P1, (K1, P1) 4 times,
K4, P1, (K1, P1) 3 times, K4*,
rep from * to * once, P1, (K1, P1)
4 times.

2nd row and every foll ws row
*K1, (P1, K1) 4 times, P4, K1,
(P1, K1) 3 times, P4*, rep from *
to * once, K1, (P1, K1) 4 times.

3rd row *P1, (K1, P1) 4 times,
C2F, P1, (K1, P1) 3 times, C2F*,
rep from * to * once, P1, (K1, P1)
4 times.

5th and 7th rows As 1st row.

8th row As 2nd row.

Rep these 8 rows until 31 rows of
rib have been worked.

Inc row Patt 17, M1, patt 12,
M1, patt 12, M1, patt 16. (60 sts)
K 1 row (this reverses cuff for turn
back).

Change to 4mm (US 5) needles
and place patt panels as foll:

1st row (rs facing) Work *1st rows
of panels* as foll: 7 sts of panel A,
then panels B, E, B, and finally
work 7 sts of panel A.

2nd row Work *2nd rows of panels* as
foll: 7 sts of panel A, then panels
B, E, B, and finally work 7 sts of
panel A.

Cont to rep the various patt rows
of each panel as required, *at the
same time*, inc 1 st at both ends of
every foll 5th row, working inc sts
into moss st at either side, until
there are 104 sts on the needle.
Now cont straight in patt until
sleeve measures 54(55:56)cm
(21¼(21¾:22)in) from cast-on
edge, ending with a ws row.
Cast off fairly loosely. Place
coloured markers 4(5:6)cm
(1½(2:2½)in) down each side
edge from cast-off edge.
Rep patt for second sleeve.

COLLAR

Join right shoulder seam.
With 3¾mm (US 4) needles and
rs facing, pick up and K 20(21:19)
sts down left front neck, 20(26:30)
sts from centre front, 21(22:20) sts
up right front neck and finally
45(48:48) sts from back neck.
(106(117:117) sts)

1st row (ws facing) K1, (P1, K1)
3 times, *P4, K1, (P1, K1) 3
times, rep from * to end.

2nd row P1, (K1, P1) 3 times,
*K4, P1, (K1, P1) 3 times, rep
from * to end.

3rd row and every foll ws row
As 1st row.

4th row P1, (K1, P1) 3 times,
*C2F, P1, (K1, P1) 3 times, rep
from * to end.

6th and 8th rows As 2nd row.

Cont in rib as set until 21 rows in
all have been worked.
Cast off fairly loosely in patt.

TO MAKE UP

Join left shoulder and collar seam.
With centre of cast-off edges of
sleeves to shoulder seams, sew
sleeves carefully into armholes,
matching coloured markers to
cast-off sts at underarm. Join side
and sleeve seams, reversing seam
for turn-back cuff.

TREE BOBBLE SWEATER

MEASUREMENTS
To fit approx age 4(6:8:10) years.
Actual measurement
61(65:72:79)cm
(24(25½:28¼:31)in).
Full length 36(40:44:48)cm
(14¼(15¾:17¼:19)in).
Sleeve seam approx
26(30:34:38)cm
(10¼(12:13½:15)in).

MATERIALS
Rowan Cabled Mercerised Cotton
50g balls.
Main colour (MC) shell pink
(328) 4(5:6:7) balls;
1st contrast colour (A) cream
(301) 1 ball;
2nd contrast colour (B) granit
(325) 1 ball.
Equivalent yarn: 3-ply.
1 pair each of 2¼mm (US 0) and
3mm (US 2) knitting needles.
Spare needle.
3 buttons.

TENSION
28 sts and 38 rows to 10cm (4in)
on 3mm (US 2) needles over patt.

SPECIAL ABBREVIATION
MB = make a bobble by knitting
3 times into next st, turn, K3,
turn, P3, turn, K3, turn, P3 tog.

NOTE
When working patt, st count
varies on some rows. *This must be
taken into account* when counting sts
during shaping. St counts given
during shapings always refer to
the original number of sts.
Shoulder opening can be worked
on either side, as preferred,
instructions given here are for
opening on left shoulder.

PATTERN
Worked over a multiple of 22 sts,
plus 11 sts.
1st row (rs facing) *P11, K11, rep
from * to last 11 sts, P11.
2nd row *K11, P11, rep from * to
last 11 sts, K11.
3rd row *P5, yon, K1, yrn, P5,
K11, rep from * to last 11 sts, P5,
yon, K1, yrn, P5.
4th row *K5, P3, K5, P11, rep
from * to last 13 sts, K5, P3, K5.
5th row *P5, K1, yf, K1, yf, K1,
P5, K5, K1 in B, K5, rep from * to
last 13 sts, P5, K1, yf, K1, yf, K1,
P5.
6th row *K5, P5, K5, P5, P1 in B,
P5, rep from * to last 15 sts, K5,
P5, K5.
7th row *P5, K2, yf, K1, yf, K2,
P5, K5, K1 in B, K5, rep from * to
last 15 sts, P5, K2, yf, K1, yf, K2,
P5.
8th row *K5, P7, K5, P5, P1 in B,
P5, rep from * to last 17 sts, K5,
P7, K5.
9th row *P5, K2, sl 1, K2 tog,
psso, K2, P5, K4, MB in A, K1 in
B, MB in A, K4, rep from * to last
17 sts, P5, K2, sl 1, K2 tog, psso,
K2, P5.
10th row As 6th row.
11th row *P5, K1, sl 1, K2 tog,
psso, K1, P5, K5, MB in A, K5,
rep from * to last 15 sts, P5, K1,
sl 1, K2 tog, psso, K1, P5.
12th row As 4th row.
13th row *P5, sl 1, K2 tog, psso,
P5, K11, rep from * to last 13 sts,
P5, sl 1, K2 tog, psso, P5.
14th row *K5, P1, K5, P11, rep
from * to last 11 sts, K5, P1, K5.
15th row As 1st row.
16th row As 2nd row.
17th row *K11, P11, rep from *
to last 11 sts, K11.
18th row *P11, K11, rep from *
to last 11 sts, P11.
19th row *K11, P5, yon, K1, yrn,
P5, rep from * to last 11 sts, K11.
20th row *P11, K5, P3, K5, rep
from * to last 11 sts, P11.
21st row *K5, K1 in B, K5, P5,
K1, yf, K1, yf, K1, P5, rep from *
to last 11 sts, K5, K1 in B, K5.
22nd row *P5, P1 in B, P5, K5,
P5, K5, rep from * to last 11 sts,
P5, P1 in B, P5.
23rd row *K5, K1 in B, K5, P5,
K2, yf, K1, yf, K2, P5, rep from *
to last 11 sts, K5, K1 in B, K5.
24th row *P5, P1 in B, P5, K5,
P7, K5, rep from * to last 11 sts,
P5, P1 in B, P5.
25th row *K4, MB in A, K1 in B,
MB in A, K4, P5, K2, sl 1, K2
tog, psso, K2, P5, rep from * to

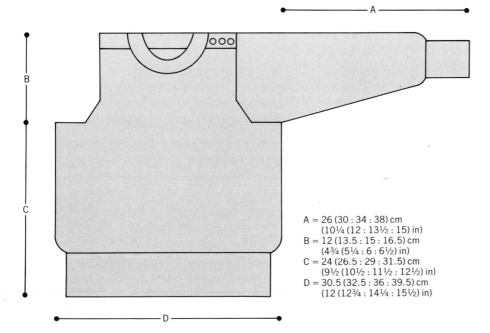

A = 26 (30 : 34 : 38) cm
(10¼ (12 : 13½ : 15) in)
B = 12 (13.5 : 15 : 16.5) cm
(4¾ (5¼ : 6 : 6½) in)
C = 24 (26.5 : 29 : 31.5) cm
(9½ (10½ : 11½ : 12½) in)
D = 30.5 (32.5 : 36 : 39.5) cm
(12 (12¾ : 14¼ : 15½) in)

last 11 sts, K4, MB in A, K1 in B, MB in A, K4.

26th row As 22nd row.

27th row *K5, MB in A, K5, P5, K1, sl 1, K2 tog, psso, K1, P5, rep from * to last 11 sts, K5, MB in A, K5.

28th row As 20th row.

29th row *K11, P5, sl 1, K2 tog, psso, P5, rep from * to last 11 sts K11.

30th row *P11, K5, P1, K5, rep from * to last 11 sts, P11.

31st row As 2nd row.

32nd row As 1st row.

These 32 rows form the patt and are rep as required.

BACK

With 2¼mm (US 0) needles and MC cast on 80(84:92:100) sts and work in K1, P1, rib for 6cm (2½in).

Inc row Rib and inc 5(7:9:11) sts evenly across row. (85(91:101:111) sts)

Change to 3mm (US 2) needles and place patt as foll:

1st row (rs facing) K 4(7:1:6), now work in patt as 1st row, K last 4(7:1:6) st(s).

2nd row P4(7:1:6), now work in patt as 2nd row, P last 4(7:1:6) st(s).

Cont in patt as now set, rep the 32 patt rows as required and working edge sts in st st and reversed st st to correspond with patt rows.

Cont straight until back measures 24(26.5:29:31.5)cm (9½(10½:11½:12½)in) from cast-on edge, ending with a ws row.

Shape armholes

Cast off 4 sts at beg of next 2 rows.

Keeping patt correct, dec 1 st at both ends of next row and every· foll alt row until 65(71:81:91) sts rem.

Now cont straight in patt until back measures 36(40:44:48)cm (14¼(15¾:17¼:19)in) from cast-on edge, ending with a ws row.

Shape shoulders and button band

Cast off 50(54:60:68) sts, and then work 6 rows in K1, P1, rib on rem 15(17:21:23) sts.

Cast off loosely ribwise.

FRONT

Work as for back until front measures 32(35.5:39:42.5)cm (12½(14:15½:16¾)in) from cast-on edge, ending with a ws row.

Shape front neck

Next row Patt 22(24:27:30) sts, turn, work 2 tog, and patt to end of row and work on this last set of 21(23:26:29) sts only.

****Keeping patt correct, dec 1 st at neck edge on every row until 15(17:21:23) sts rem.

Now cont straight until front measures same as back to cast-off shoulder edge (ignoring button band) ending at armhole edge.

Buttonhole band

Work on these 15(17:21:23) sts in K1, P1, rib for 2 rows.

Buttonhole row Rib 3(4:6:7), cast off 2 sts, rib 5, cast off 2 sts, rib to end.

Next row Rib, casting on 2 sts over cast-off sts on previous row. (2 buttonholes made.)

Work 2 more rows in rib, then cast off loosely ribwise.

Return to rem sts and slip centre 21(23:27:31) sts onto a spare needle, with rs facing rejoin yarn to rem sts and patt to end of row.

Next row Patt to last 2 sts, work 2 tog.

Now work as for first side from ** to end, and working 6 rows in rib, but omit buttonholes.

SLEEVES

With 2¼mm (US 0) needles and MC cast on 54 sts and work in K1, P1, rib for 6cm (2½in).

Inc row Rib and inc 9(13:17:23) sts evenly across row. (63(67:71:77) sts)

Change to 3mm (US 2) needles and place patt as foll:

1st row (rs facing) K4(6:8:0), now work in patt as 1st row, K last 4(6:8:0) sts.

Cont straight in patt as set, rep the 32 patt rows as for back until sleeve measures approx 26(30:34:38)cm (10¼(12:13½:15)in) from cast-on edge, ending with a ws row and same section of patt as back/front to beg of armhole shaping.

Shape top

Cast off 4 sts at beg of next 2 rows.

Keeping patt correct dec 1 st at both ends of next row and every foll alt row until 31 sts rem.

Now dec 1 st at both ends of every row until 9 sts rem.

Cast off fairly loosely.

Rep patt for second sleeve.

NECKBAND

Join right front shoulder ribbing to cast-off sts of back shoulder.

With 2¼mm (US 0) needles and rs facing and MC, pick up and K20(22:24:26) sts down left front neck including top of buttonhole band, then K across centre front sts, pick up and K20(22:24:26) sts up right front neck, and 35(37:39:41) sts across back neck and button band. (96(104:114:124) sts)

Work in K1, P1, rib for 2 rows.

Buttonhole row (ws facing) Rib to last 5 sts, cast off 2 sts, rib to end.

Next row Rib casting on 2 sts over cast-off sts on previous row.

Rib 2 more rows.

Cast off loosely ribwise.

TO MAKE UP

Place front buttonhole band over back button band and catch st in position at armhole edge. Join side and sleeve seams. Sew sleeves into armholes, easing to fit. Sew on buttons to correspond with buttonholes.

ROSEBUD SWEATER

This sweater was inspired by the fabric of the skirt that my daughter Shebah is wearing in the photograph: a beautiful Italian silk crêpe de chine printed with tiny pink rosebuds. Usually things work the other way round: I design a sweater first, decide what yarn colours I want and then go to the fabric fairs to order some matching cloth. The Italians make the most beautiful silks in the world; they have the best colours and often the best designs.

MEASUREMENTS

One size only to fit bust 86–97cm (34–38in).
Actual measurement 115cm (45¼in).
Full length 45cm (17¾in).
Sleeve seam 45cm (17¾in).

MATERIALS

Rowan Handknit D.K. Cotton 50g balls.
Main colour (MC) turkish plum (277) 12 balls;
1st contrast colour (A) fuchsia (272) 2 balls;
2nd contrast colour (B) ecru (251) 1 ball;
3rd contrast colour (C) cherry (298) 1 ball;
4th contrast colour (D) clover (266) 1 ball.
Equivalent yarn: D.K.
1 pair each of 3¾mm (US 4) and 4mm (US 5) knitting needles.
One 3¾mm (US 4) short circular needle.
2 spare needles.

TENSION

20 sts and 28 rows to 10cm (4in) on 4mm (US 5) needles over st st.
See page 10.

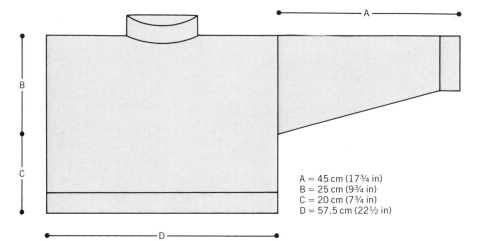

A = 45 cm (17¾ in)
B = 25 cm (9¾ in)
C = 20 cm (7¾ in)
D = 57.5 cm (22½ in)

BACK

With 3¾mm (US 4) needles and MC cast on 112 sts and work in K2, P2, rib for 5cm (2in).
Inc row Rib and inc 3 sts evenly across row. (115 sts)
Change to 4mm (US 5) needles and starting with a K row work in st st from *back chart* until 103 rows have been worked.
Shape back neck
Next row (ws facing) Patt 46, turn, work 2 tog and patt to end of row and work on this last set of 45 sts only.
**Keeping chart correct dec 1 st

at neck edge on every row until 40 sts rem. Cast off.
Return to rem sts and sl centre 23 sts on a spare needle, with ws facing rejoin yarn to rem sts and patt to end of row.
Next row Patt to last 2 sts, work 2 tog.
Now work as for first side from ** to end.

FRONT

Work as for back until 95 rows of patt have been worked.
Shape front neck
Next row (ws facing) Patt 47, turn, work 2 tog and patt to end

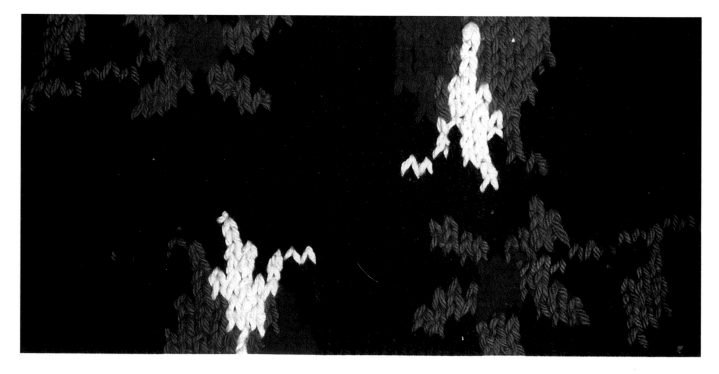

of row and work on this last set of
46 sts only.
***Keeping chart correct dec
1 st at neck edge on every row
until 41 sts rem, then dec once
more on this edge on foll 4th
row. (40 sts) Work straight
until chart is complete.
Cast off.
Return to rem sts and sl centre
21 sts on a spare needle, with ws

facing rejoin yarn to rem sts and
patt to end of row.
Next row Patt to last 2 sts,
work 2 tog.
Now work as for first side from
*** to end.

SLEEVES
With 3¾mm (US 4) needles and
MC, cast on 48 sts and work in
K2, P2, rib for 5cm (2in).

Inc row Rib and inc 10 sts evenly
across row. (58 sts)
Change to 4mm (US 5) needles
and starting with a K row
work in st st foll *sleeve chart, at
the same time*, inc 1 st at both ends
of every foll 5th row as shown,
until there are 100 sts on the
needle.
Now cont straight until the chart
is complete.

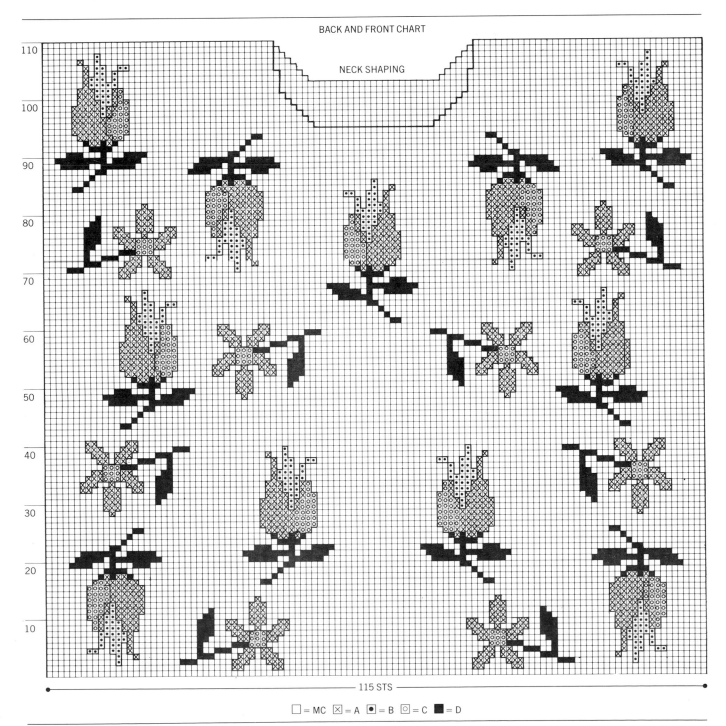

BACK AND FRONT CHART

NECK SHAPING

115 STS

□ = MC ☒ = A ◉ = B ◎ = C ■ = D

SLEEVE CHART

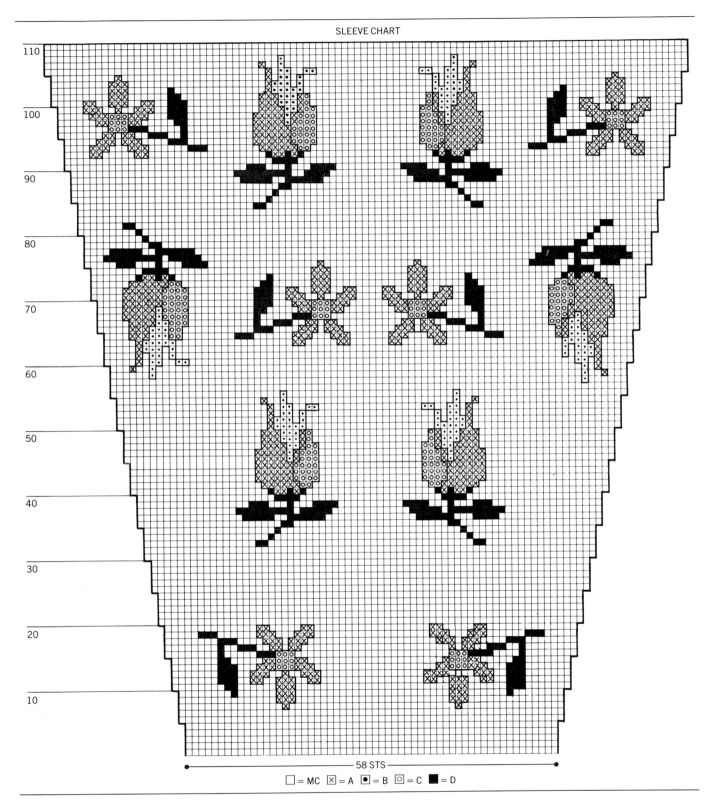

58 STS

□ = MC ☒ = A ● = B ⊙ = C ■ = D

Cast off fairly loosely.
Rep patt for second sleeve.

NECKBAND
Join both shoulder seams.
With the 3¾mm (US 4) circular
needle and MC and rs facing, pick
up and K 36 sts around back neck
and 44 sts around front neck
including sts on spare needles.
(80 sts)
Work in rounds of K2, P2, rib for
5cm (2in).
Cast off fairly loosely ribwise.

TO MAKE UP
With centre of cast-off edges of
sleeves to shoulder seams, sew
sleeves carefully in position
reaching down to same depth on
front and back. Join side and
sleeve seams.

1930'S
FAIR ISLE

This Fair Isle sweater, knitted in silk and wool, is a very versatile garment to own. The colourway I have used is soft and muted, in the classic colours that American stores especially like. Changing the colourway in Fair Isles to bright colours on black or pastels on cream produces a completely different-looking finished garment.

MEASUREMENTS

To fit bust 86(91:97)cm
(34(36:38)in).
Actual measurement
96(101:106)cm
(37¾(39¾:41¾)in).
Full length 71cm (28in).
Sleeve seam approx 45cm
(17¾in).

MATERIALS

Rowan Silk and Wool 25g balls.
Main colour (MC)
camel (851) 11(12:13) balls;
1st contrast colour (A)
moss green (852) 2(2:2) balls;
2nd contrast colour (B)
chocolate (853) 3(3:3) balls;
3rd contrast colour (C)
black (840) 5(5:5) balls;
4th contrast colour (D)
oatmeal (854) 2(2:2) balls;
5th contrast colour (E)
coral (855) 2(2:2) balls;
6th contrast colour (F)
donkey (856) 2(2:2) balls.
Equivalent yarn: 4-ply.
1 pair each of 2¼mm (US 0) and
3¼mm (US 3) knitting needles.
4 spare needles.

TENSION

32 sts and 32 rows to 10cm (4in)
on 3¼mm (US 3) needles over
Fair Isle patt. See page 10.

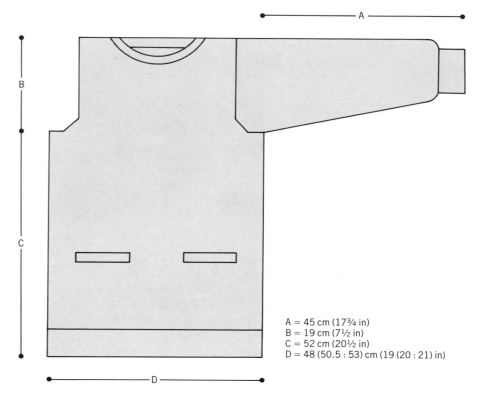

A = 45 cm (17¾ in)
B = 19 cm (7½ in)
C = 52 cm (20½ in)
D = 48 (50.5 : 53) cm (19 (20 : 21) in)

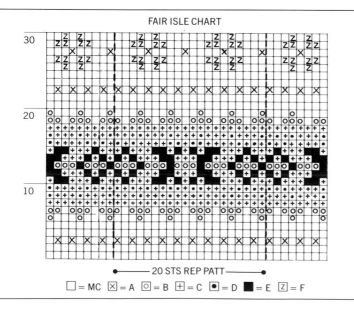

FAIR ISLE CHART

20 STS REP PATT

☐ = MC ☒ = A ⊡ = B ⊞ = C ⬤ = D ■ = E Ⓩ = F

BACK

With 2¼mm (US 0) needles and
MC cast on 152(160:168) sts and
work in K1, P1, rib for 6cm
(2½in), inc 1 st on last row.
(153(161:169) sts)
Change to 3¼mm (US 3) needles
and starting with a K row work in
st st from chart as foll:
1st row (rs facing) Work 6(0:4)
sts before the dotted line, rep the
20 st patt to last 7(1:5) st(s), work
7(1:5) st(s) beyond the dotted
line.
2nd row Work 7(1:5) st(s) before
the dotted line, rep the 20 st patt
to last 6(0:4) sts, work 6(0:4) sts
beyond the dotted line.
The chart is now set. Cont to rep
the 30 rows of chart as required
and work straight until back
measures 52cm (20½in) from
cast-on edge ending with a ws
row.

Shape armholes

Cast off 10 sts at beg of next 2
rows.
Keeping patt correct, dec 1 st at
both ends of every row until
115(121:127) sts rem. Now dec 1
st at both ends of every foll alt row
until 105(111:117) sts rem.
Now cont straight until back
measures 71cm (28in) from
cast-on edge, ending with a ws
row.

Shape shoulders

Keeping patt correct cast off
29(31:33) sts at beg of next
2 rows.
Leave rem 47(49:51) sts on a
spare needle.

POCKET LINING

With 3¼mm (US 3) needles and MC cast on 40 sts and starting with a K row work straight in st st for 50 rows, thus ending with a ws row.

Leave sts on a spare needle.

Rep patt for second pocket lining.

FRONT

Work as for back until 50 patt rows have been worked, thus ending with a ws row.

Place pockets

Next row Patt 19(20:21), *place next 40 sts onto a spare needle and in their place patt across the 40 sts from first pocket lining*, patt next 35(41:47) sts, then rep from * to * once more working across sts of second pocket lining, patt to end of row.

Cont in patt as set across all sts, working armholes as for back, and cont straight until front measures 64cm (25¼in) from cast-on edge, ending with a ws row.

Shape front neck

Next row Patt 37(40:43), turn, work 2 tog, and patt to end of row and cont on this last set of 36(39:42) sts only.

**Keeping patt correct, dec 1 st at neck edge on every row until 29(31:33) sts rem.

Now cont straight until front measures same as back to cast-off shoulder edge, ending at side edge. Cast off.

Return to rem sts and sl centre 31 sts onto a spare needle, with rs facing rejoin yarn to rem sts and patt to end of row.

Next row Work to last 2 sts, work 2 tog.

Now work as for first side from ** to end.

SLEEVES

With 2¼mm (US 0) needles and MC cast on 62 sts and work in K1, P1, rib for 6cm (2½in).

Inc row Rib and inc 39 sts evenly

across row. (101 sts)

Change to 3¼mm (US 3) needles and starting with a K row work in st st from chart as foll:

1st row (rs facing) Work 0 sts before the dotted line, rep the 20 st patt to last st, work 1 st beyond the dotted line.

The chart is now set. Cont straight until sleeve measures approx 45cm (17¾in) from cast-on edge, ending on same patt row as back/front to beg of armhole shaping.

Shape top

Cast off 10 sts at beg of next 2 rows.

Keeping patt correct, dec 1 st at beg of next 16 rows.

Work 18 rows straight.

Now dec 1 st at both ends of next 6 rows.

Cast off 2 sts at beg of foll 4 rows.

Cast off 3 sts at beg of next 4 rows.

Next row K1, (K2 tog) across row.

Cast off.

Rep patt for second sleeve.

POCKET TOPS

With 2¼mm (US 0) needles and MC and rs facing, work across one set of sts on spare needle in K1, P1, rib for 7 rows.

Cast off fairly loosely ribwise.

NECKBAND

Join right shoulder seam.

With 2¼mm (US 0) needles and rs facing and MC, pick up and K 34 sts down left front neck, K across centre front sts, pick up and K 34 sts up right front neck and finally K across centre back sts. (146(148:150) sts)

Work in K1, P1, rib for 7 rows.

Cast off fairly loosely ribwise.

Join left shoulder and neckband seam.

TO MAKE UP

Join side and sleeve seams carefully matching patt. Set sleeves into armholes gathering fullness across top of shoulder. Catch down side edges of pocket tops and sl st pocket linings neatly in position on wrong side.

EMBROIDERED SWEATER

The embroidery on this sweater is fairly simple using four basic stitches to create small flowers within the diamond shapes. You could make it without the flowers if you like, but I think they are very effective. The colours could be changed to pastels on white or bright colours on black. It is a classically shaped sweater that is especially popular with our American customers.

MEASUREMENTS

To fit bust 86(91:97)cm
(34(36:38)in).
Actual measurement
96(100:105)cm
(37¾(39¼:41¼)in).
Full length 56(57:58)cm
(22(22½:23)in).
Sleeve seam 45cm (17¾in).

MATERIALS

Rowan Silk and Wool 25g balls.
Ecru (857) 20(20:21) balls.
For embroidery: small amounts
of same wool in emerald (850);
red (842); purple (841); and
gold (847).
Rowan Botany Wool 25g hanks.
For embroidery: small amount in
peacock (633).
Equivalent yarn: 4-ply.
1 pair each of 2¼mm (US 0) and
3¼mm (US 3) knitting needles.
One 2¼mm (US 0) short circular
needle.
2 spare needles.

TENSION

28 sts and 36 rows to 10cm (4in)
on 3¼mm (US 3) needles over
st st. See page 10.

SPECIAL ABBREVIATION

MB = make bobble by knitting 4
times into next st as foll:
K1, P1, K1, P1, turn, K4, turn,
P4, turn, K4, turn, P4 tog.

BACK

With 2¼mm (US 0) needles cast
on 130(134:138) sts and work in
K1, P1, rib for 10cm (4in).
Inc row Rib and inc 5(7:9) sts
evenly across row.
(135(141:147) sts)
Change to 3¼mm (US 3) needles
and work in patt as foll:
1st row (rs facing) K37(40:43),
MB, *P1, K18, MB, rep from * to
last 37(40:43) sts, P1, K36(39:42).
2nd row and every foll alt row
P.
3rd row K35(38:41), MB, P1,

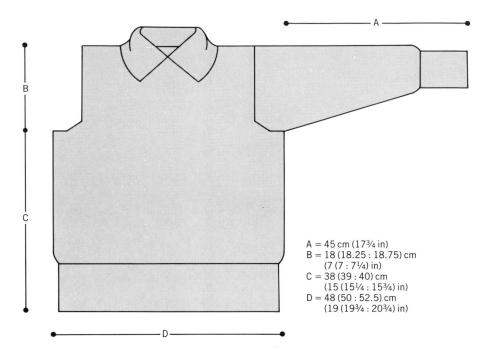

A = 45 cm (17¾ in)
B = 18 (18.25 : 18.75) cm
(7 (7 : 7¼) in)
C = 38 (39 : 40) cm
(15 (15¼ : 15¾) in)
D = 48 (50 : 52.5) cm
(19 (19¾ : 20¾) in)

*K2, MB, P1, K14, MB, P1, rep
from * to last 38(41:44) sts, K2,
MB, P1, K34(37:40).
5th row K33(36:39), MB, *P1,
K6, MB, P1, K10, MB, rep from *
to last 41(44:47) sts, P1, K6, MB,
P1, K32(35:38).
7th row K31(34:37), MB, *P1,
K10, MB, P1, K6, MB, rep from *
to last 43(46:49) sts, P1, K10,
MB, P1, K30(33:36).
9th row K29(32:35), MB, *P1,
K14, MB, P1, K2, MB, rep from *
to last 45(48:51) sts, P1, K14,
MB, P1, K28(31:34).
11th row K27(30:33), MB, *P1,
K18, MB, rep from * to last
27(30:33) sts, P1, K26(29:32).
13th row As 9th row.
15th row As 7th row.
17th row As 5th row.
19th row As 3rd row.
20th row P.
These 20 rows form the patt and
are rep as required. Cont straight
in patt until back measures
38(39:40)cm (15(15¼:15¾)in)
from cast-on edge, ending with a
ws row.
Shape armholes
Cast off 8 sts at beg of next 2 rows.
Next row K1, K2 tog, patt to last
3 sts, K2 tog tbl, K1.

Next row K1, P2 tog, patt to last
3 sts, P2 tog, K1.
Rep last 2 rows until 101(107:111)
sts rem.
Now cont straight until back
measures 56(57:58)cm
(22(22½:23)in) from cast-on
edge, ending with a ws row.
Shape shoulders
Cast off 28(30:31) sts at beg of
next 2 rows. Leave rem 45(47:49)
sts on a spare needle.

FRONT

Work as for back until front
measures 51(52:53)cm
(20(20½:21)in) from cast-on
edge, ending with a ws row.
Shape front neck
Next row Patt 36(38:40), turn,
work 2 tog and patt to end of row
and work on this last set of
35(37:39) sts only.
**Keeping patt correct dec 1 st at
neck edge on every row until
28(30:31) sts rem.
Now cont straight until front
measures same as back to cast-off
shoulder edge ending at armhole
edge. Cast off.
Return to rem sts and slip centre
29(31:31) sts onto a spare needle,
with rs facing rejoin yarn to rem

sts and patt to end of row.
Next row Patt to last 2 sts, work 2 tog.
Now work as for first side from ** to end.

SLEEVES
With 2¼mm (US 0) needles cast on 62(64:66) sts and work in K1, P1, rib for 10cm (4in).
Inc row Rib and inc 6(8:10) sts evenly across row. (68(72:76) sts)
Change to 3¼mm (US 3) needles and work in patt as foll:
1st row (rs facing) K23(25:27), MB, P1, K18, MB, P1, K to end.
2nd row and every foll alt row P.
3rd row K25(27:29), MB, P1, K14, MB, P1, K to end.
5th row K27(29:31), MB, P1, K10, MB, P1, K to end.
7th row K29(31:33), MB, P1, K6, MB, P1, K to end.
9th row K31(33:35), MB, P1, K2, MB, P1, K to end.
11th row K33(35:37), MB, P1,

K to end.
13th row As 9th row.
15th row As 7th row.
17th row As 5th row.
19th row As 3rd row.
20th row P.
The patt for the sleeves is now set. Cont to rep the 20 rows as required, *at the same time*, inc 1 st at both ends of every foll 6th row until there are 100(104:106) sts on the needle working inc sts into st st at either side.
Now cont straight until sleeve measures 45cm (17¾in) from cast-on edge ending with a ws row.
Shape top
Cast off 8 sts at beg of next 2 rows. Now dec 1 st at both ends of next row and every foll alt row until 38(40:42) sts rem, then dec 1 st at both ends of every row until 22(22:24) sts rem.
Next row K 2 tog across row. Cast off.
Rep patt for second sleeve.

COLLAR
Join both shoulder seams.
With the 2¼mm (US 0) circular needle and rs facing, pick up and K 28 sts down left front neck, K across centre front sts, pick up and K 28 sts up right front neck and finally K across centre back sts.
(130(134:136) sts)
Work in rounds of K1, P1, rib for 6 rounds, ending at centre front.
Divide for collar
Next row Rib to centre front, turn, and work backwards and forwards in rows of K1, P1, rib until collar measures 8cm (3in) from division.
Cast off loosely ribwise.

TO MAKE UP
Join side and sleeve seams. Set sleeves into armholes gathering any fullness evenly across top of shoulder. Turn collar over to right side.

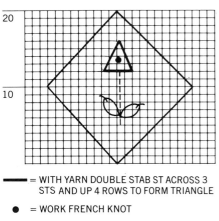

EMBROIDERY DIAGRAM

━━ = WITH YARN DOUBLE STAB ST ACROSS 3 STS AND UP 4 ROWS TO FORM TRIANGLE

● = WORK FRENCH KNOT

- - - = WORK STEM ST

⟋ = WORK LAZY DAISY ST

EMBROIDERY
Foll embroidery diagram and work flowers in centre of each diamond panel of front and back following colour sequence as shown in the photograph or making up your own. Fasten off each flower securely.

BORDER-PATTERN SWEATER

Sweaters with this simple, loose, square shape are very popular with my customers because they are so comfortable and easy to wear, perfect for lazy weekends. The straightforward abstract patterns on this sweater, which was designed for the same collection as the Abstract Floral Sweater shown on page 48, looks equally good on a black background with either jewel or bright colours as contrasts.

MEASUREMENTS
One size only to fit bust
86–102cm (34–40in).
Actual measurement
126cm (49½in).
Full length 70cm (27½in).
Sleeve seam 40cm (15¾in).

MATERIALS
Rowan Handknit D.K. Cotton
50g balls.
Main colour (MC) ecru (251)
16 balls;
1st contrast colour (A) taupe
(253) 2 balls;
2nd contrast colour (B) black
(252) 3 balls.
Rowan Cotton Chenille
100g hanks.
3rd contrast colour (C) french
mustard (363) 1 hank.
Rowan Fine Cotton Chenille
50g balls (used double).
4th contrast colour (D) lacquer
(388) 2 balls.
Equivalent yarn: D.K. used
throughout.
1 pair each of 3¾mm (US 4) and
4mm (US 5) knitting needles.
2 spare needles.

TENSION
20 sts and 28 rows to 10cm (4in)
on 4mm (US 5) needles over st st
using MC. See page 10.

BACK
With 3¾mm (US 4) needles and
MC, cast on 120 sts and work in
K2, P2, rib for 5cm (2in).
Change to 4mm (US 5) needles
and starting with a K row work in
st st from chart, rep the 20 st patt
6 times across row. Cont foll chart
until the 76 rows are complete, *at
the same time*, inc 1 st at both ends
of 50th and 76th rows.
Now rep rows 51–76 for the rem of
the back, and inc 1 st at each end
of 102nd row. (126 sts)
Now cont straight foll chart, rep
the 26 rows as required until back
measures 68cm (26¾in) from

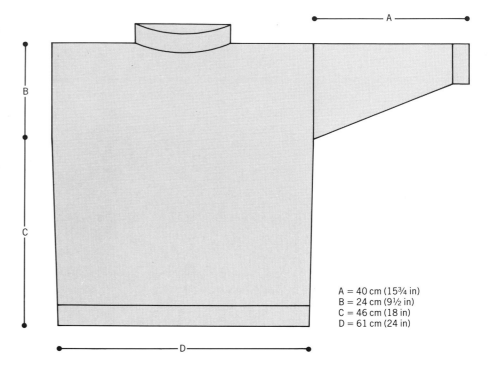

A = 40 cm (15¾ in)
B = 24 cm (9½ in)
C = 46 cm (18 in)
D = 61 cm (24 in)

cast-on edge, ending with a ws
row.
Shape back neck
Next row Patt 45, sl next 36 sts
onto a spare needle, patt to end
and cont on this last set of 45 sts
only.
***Keeping patt correct, dec 1 st
at neck edge on every row until 40
sts rem.**
Cast off.
With ws facing rejoin yarn to rem

sts and work as for first side from
*** to end.

FRONT
Work as for back until front
measures 65cm (25½in) from
cast-on edge, ending with a ws
row.
Shape front neck
Work as for back from ** to **.
****Now cont straight until front
measures same as back to cast-off
shoulder edge, ending on same
patt row.
Cast off.
With ws facing rejoin yarn to rem
sts and work as for back from ***
to **. Now work as for first side
from **** to end.

SLEEVES
With 3¾mm (US 4) needles and
MC, cast on 48 sts and work in
K2, P2, rib for 5cm (2in), on last
row inc 1 st at both ends. (50 sts)
Change to 4mm (US 5) needles
and starting with a K row work in
st st from chart as foll:
1st row (rs facing) Work 5 sts
before the dotted line, rep the 20
st patt twice, work 5 sts beyond
the dotted line.

BORDER PATTERN CHART

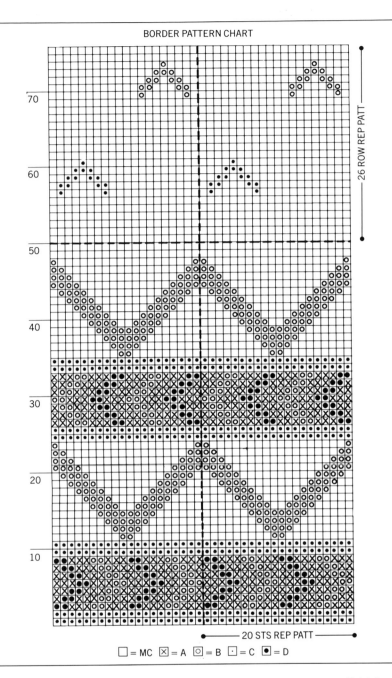

□ = MC ☒ = A ⊡ = B ⊡ = C ⊙ = D

The chart is now placed. Cont to rep the patt rows as for back, *at the same time*, inc 1 st at both ends of every foll 3rd row until there are 96 sts on the needle, working inc sts into the patt.

Now cont straight until sleeve measures 40cm (15¾in) from cast-on edge, ending with a ws row.

Cast off fairly loosely.

Rep patt for second sleeve.

NECKBAND

Join right shoulder seam.

With 4mm (US 5) needles and rs facing and MC, pick up and K 9 sts down left front neck, K across the centre front sts, pick up and K 9 sts up right front neck, 5 sts down right back neck, K across centre back sts and finally pick up and K 5 sts up left back neck. (100 sts)

Next row In C, P.

Now starting with a K row, work in st st from chart, rep the 20 st patt 5 times across, *but* start chart on 2nd row and read K rows from left to right and P rows from right

to left. Cont as set until 11th row has been worked, now cont in st st in MC only for 12 rows.

Cast off fairly loosely.

TO MAKE UP

Join left shoulder and neckband seam. Fold neckband in half to wrong side and sl st loosely in position. With centre of cast-off edges of sleeves to shoulder seams, sew sleeves carefully in position reaching down to same depth on front and back. Join side and sleeve seams matching patts.

FAIR ISLES IN PRIMARY COLOURS

The first time I ever knitted a garment myself was when my daughter Shebah was a baby. Her coats, hats and jumpers were so brightly coloured that people would stop me in the street to ask where I had bought them. I like to see children in vivid colours. This Fair Isle sweater can be knitted with or without pockets and collar. People often buy the smaller-sized children's Fair Isles as an unusual but much-appreciated christening present.

FAIR ISLE
IN PRIMARY COLOURS

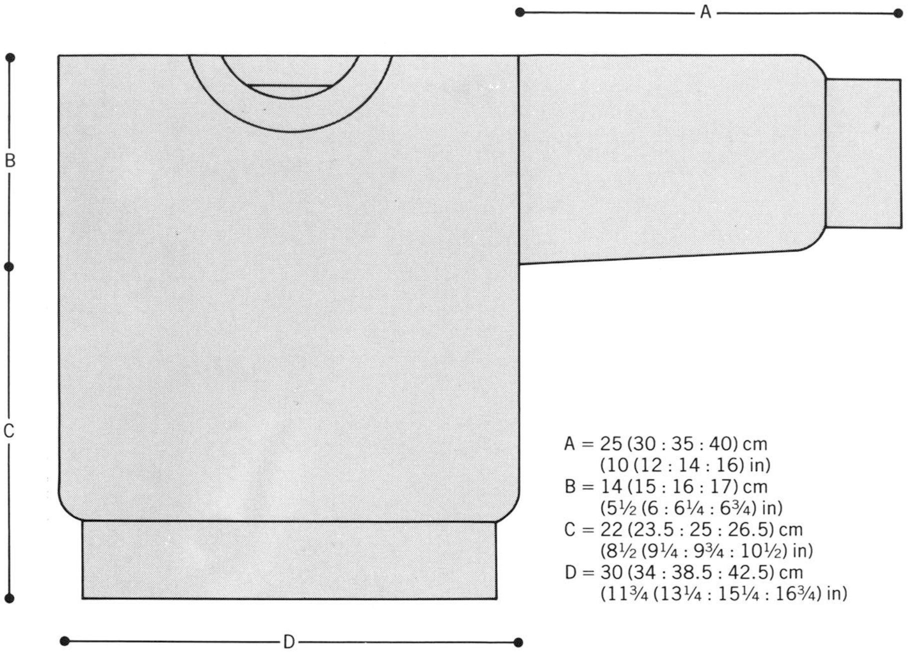

MEASUREMENTS
To fit approx age
4–5(6–7:8–9:10–11) years.
Actual measurement
60(68:77:85)cm
(23½(26¾:30¼:33½)in).
Full length 36(38.5:41:43.5)cm
(14(15:16:17)in).
Sleeve seam 25(30:35:40)cm
(10(12:14:16)in).

MATERIALS
Rowan Lightweight D.K. Wool
25g hanks.
Main colour (MC) navy (97)
12(12:13:13) hanks;
1st contrast colour (A) yellow (12)
2(2:3:3) hanks;
2nd contrast colour (B) red (115)
2(2:3:3) hanks;
3rd contrast colour (C) fuchsia
(96) 2(2:2:2) hanks;
4th contrast colour (D) emerald
(124) 2(2:2:2) hanks;
5th contrast colour (E) purple
(126) 2(2:2:2) hanks.
Equivalent yarn: D.K.
1 pair each of 3mm (US 2) and
3¼mm (US 3) knitting needles.
2 spare needles.

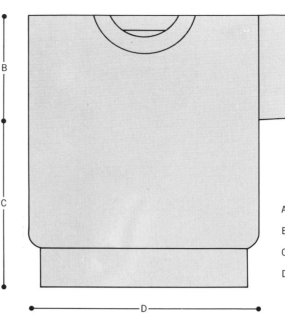

A = 25 (30 : 35 : 40) cm
    (10 (12 : 14 : 16) in)
B = 14 (15 : 16 : 17) cm
    (5½ (6 : 6¼ : 6¾) in)
C = 22 (23.5 : 25 : 26.5) cm
    (8½ (9¼ : 9¾ : 10½) in)
D = 30 (34 : 38.5 : 42.5) cm
    (11¾ (13¼ : 15¼ : 16¾) in)

TENSION
28 sts and 34 rows to 10cm (4in)
on 3¼mm (US 3) needles over
Fair Isle patt. See page 10.

BACK
With 3mm (US 2) needles and
MC, cast on 74(86:98:110) sts and
work in K1, P1, rib for 5cm (2in).
Inc row Rib and inc 10 sts evenly
across row. (84(96:108:120) sts)
Change to 3¼mm (US 3) needles
and starting with a K row work in

st st from chart, rep the 12 st patt
7(8:9:10) times across row.
Cont as now set and rep the 60
rows of chart as required until
back measures 36(38.5:41:43.5)cm
(14(15:16:17)in) from cast-on
edge ending with a ws row.
Shape shoulders
Keeping patt correct cast off
24(28:32:36) sts at beg of next 2
rows.
Leave rem 36(40:44:48) sts on a
spare needle.

FRONT
Work as for back until front
measures 31(33:35:37)cm
(12¼(13:13¾:14½)in) from
cast-on edge ending with a ws
row.
Shape front neck
Next row Patt 32(36:40:44), turn,
work 2 tog, patt to end of row and
cont on this last set of
31(35:39:43) sts only.
**Keeping patt correct dec 1 st at
neck edge on every row until
24(28:32:36) sts rem. Now cont
straight until front measures same
as back to cast-off shoulder edge,
ending at side edge. Cast off.
Return to rem sts and sl centre

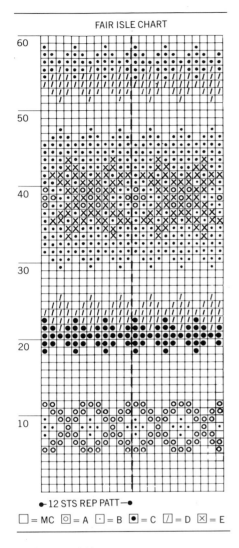

FAIR ISLE CHART

●—12 STS REP PATT—●

□ = MC   ◎ = A   · = B   ● = C   ╱ = D   ☒ = E

20(24:28:32) sts onto a spare
needle, with rs facing rejoin yarn
to rem sts and patt to end of row.
Next row Patt to last 2 sts,
work 2 tog.
Now work as for first side from **
to end.

SLEEVES

With 3mm (US 2) needles and
MC cast on 48 sts and work in
K1, P1, rib for 5cm (2in).
Inc row Rib and inc 12 sts evenly
across row. (60 sts)
Change to 3¼mm (US 3) needles
and starting with a K row work in
st st from chart, rep the 12 st patt
5 times across row. Cont as now
set and rep the 60 rows of chart as
required, *at the same time*, inc 1 st at
both ends of every foll 6th row
until there are 80(86:92:96) sts on
the needle, working inc sts into
patt.
Now cont straight until sleeve
measures 25(30:35:40)cm
(10(12:14:16)in) from cast-on
edge, ending with a ws row.
Cast off fairly loosely.
Rep patt for second sleeve.

NECKBAND

Join right shoulder seam.
With 3mm (US 2) needles and
MC and rs facing, pick up and K
16(18:20:22) sts down left front
neck, K across centre front sts,
pick up and K 16(18:20:22) sts up
right front neck and finally K
across centre back sts.
(88(100:112:124) sts)
Work in K1, P1, rib for 6 rows.
Cast off fairly loosely ribwise.

TO MAKE UP

Join left shoulder and neckband
seam. With centre of cast-off
edges of sleeves to shoulder seams
sew sleeves carefully in position
reaching down to same depth on
front and back. Join side and
sleeve seams.

LONG
FAIR ISLE
IN PRIMARY COLOURS

MEASUREMENTS
To fit approx age
4–5(6–7:8–9:10–11) years.
Actual measurement
60(68:77:85)cm
(23½(26¾:30¼:33½)in).
Full length 46(52:58:60)cm
(18(20½:23:23¾)in).
Sleeve seam 25(30:35:40)cm
(10(12:14:16)in).

MATERIALS
Rowan Lightweight D.K. Wool
25g hanks.
Main colour (MC) navy (97)
13(13:14:14) hanks;
1st contrast colour (A) yellow (12)
3(3:4:4) hanks;
2nd contrast colour (B) red (115)
3(3:4:4) hanks;
3rd contrast colour (C) fuchsia
(96) 3(3:3:3) hanks;
4th contrast colour (D) emerald
(124) 3(3:3:3) hanks;
5th contrast colour (E) purple
(126) 3(3:3:3) hanks.
Equivalent yarn: D.K.
1 pair each of 3mm (US 2) and
3¼mm (US 3) knitting needles.
4 spare needles.
One 3mm (US 2) short circular
needle.

TENSION
28 sts and 34 rows to 10cm (4in)
on 3¼mm (US 3) needles over
Fair Isle patt. See page 10.

CHART NOTE
The chart for this patt is the same
as the chart for Fair Isle in
Primary Colours (see page 99).

BACK
With 3mm (US 2) needles and
MC, cast on 84(96:108:120) sts
and work in K1, P1, rib for
5cm (2in).

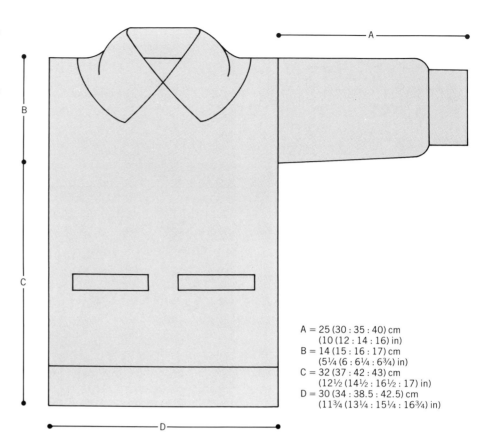

A = 25 (30 : 35 : 40) cm
(10 (12 : 14 : 16) in)
B = 14 (15 : 16 : 17) cm
(5¼ (6 : 6¼ : 6¾) in)
C = 32 (37 : 42 : 43) cm
(12½ (14½ : 16½ : 17) in)
D = 30 (34 : 38.5 : 42.5) cm
(11¾ (13¼ : 15¼ : 16¾) in)

Change to 3¼mm (US 3) needles
and starting with a K row work in
st st from chart, rep the 12 st patt
7(8:9:10) times across row.
Cont as now set and rep the 60
rows of chart as required until
back measures 46(52:58:60)cm
(18(20½:23:23¾)in) from cast-on
edge ending with a ws row.
Shape shoulders
Keeping patt correct cast off
24(28:32:36) sts at beg of next 2
rows.
Leave rem 36(40:44:48) sts on a
spare needle.

POCKET LININGS
With 3¼mm (US 3) needles and
MC, cast on 28(28:34:34) sts and
starting with a K row work in st st
for 34(34:48:48) rows, thus ending
with a ws row.
Leave sts on a spare needle.
Rep patt for second pocket lining.

FRONT
Work as for back until
34(34:48:48) rows of chart have

been worked, thus ending with a
ws row.
Place pockets
Next row Patt 5(11:10:16),
*place next 28(28:34:34) sts on a
spare needle and in their place
patt across the 28(28:34:34) sts of
first pocket lining*, patt next
18(18:20:20) sts, then rep from *
to * once more working across sts
of second pocket lining, patt to
end of row.
Cont in patt as set across all sts
until front measures 42(47.5:53:
54.5)cm (16½(18¾:21:21½)in)
from cast-on edge, ending with a
ws row.
Shape front neck
Next row Patt 34(38:42:46),
turn, work 2 tog, patt to end of
row and cont on this last set of
33(37:41:45) sts only.
**Keeping patt correct dec 1 st at
neck edge on every row until
24(28:32:36) sts rem. Now cont
straight until front measures same
as back to cast-off shoulder edge,
ending at side edge. Cast off.

Return to rem sts and slip centre 16(20:24:28) sts on a spare needle, with rs facing rejoin yarn to rem sts and patt to end of row.
Next row Work to last 2 sts, work 2 tog.
Now work as for first side from ** to end.

SLEEVES

With 3mm (US 2) needles and MC cast on 48 sts and work in K1, P1, rib for 5cm (2in).
Inc row Rib and inc 12 sts evenly across row. (60 sts)
Change to 3¼mm (US 3) needles and starting with a K row work in st st from chart, rep the 12 st patt 5 times across row.
Cont as now set and rep the 60 rows of chart as required, *at the same time*, inc 1 st at both ends of every foll 6th row until there are 80(86:92:96) sts on the needle,

working inc sts into the patt.
Now cont straight until sleeve measures 25(30:35:40)cm (10(12:14:16)in) from cast-on edge, ending with a ws row.
Cast off fairly loosely.
Rep patt for second sleeve.

COLLAR

Join both shoulder seams.
With the 3mm (US 2) circular needle and MC and rs facing, pick up and K15(17:19:21) sts down left front neck, K across centre front sts, pick up and K15(17:19:21) sts up right front neck and finally K across centre back sts. (82(94:106:118)sts)
Work in rounds of K1, P1, rib for 6 rounds, ending at centre front.
Divide for collar
Next row Rib to centre front, turn, and work backwards and

forwards in rows of K1, P1, rib until collar measures 8cm (3in) from division.
Cast off loosely ribwise.

POCKET TOPS

With 3mm (US 2) needles and MC and rs facing, work across one set of sts on spare needle in K1, P1, rib for 6 rows.
Cast off fairly loosely ribwise.

TO MAKE UP

With centre of cast-off edges of sleeves to shoulder seams, sew sleeves carefully in position reaching down to same depth on front and back. Join side and sleeve seams. Catch down side edges of pocket tops and sl st pocket linings neatly in position on wrong side. Turn collar over to right side.

TAPESTRY SWEATER

A particular favourite of mine, this sweater is very difficult to knit because of all the colour changes. If you want to simplify things, the centres of the flowers and leaves could be Swiss embroidered on afterwards. The idea came from a beautiful piece of floral tapestry that I found in an antique shop in Paris: I think it was originally a furnishing fabric! The sweater also looks good with the same colours on a black background.

MEASUREMENTS

One size only to fit bust
86–102cm (34–40in).
Actual measurement
122cm (48in).
Full length 75cm (29½in).
Sleeve seam (with cuff turned
down) 47cm (18½in).

MATERIALS

Rowan Lightweight D.K. Wool
25g hanks.
Main colour (MC) cream (2)
30 hanks;
1st contrast colour (A) leaf green
(407) 3 hanks;
2nd contrast colour (B) mustard
(72) 2 hanks.
Rowan Fine Cotton Chenille
50g balls (used double).
3rd contrast colour (C) cyclamen
(385) 2 balls;
4th contrast colour (D) cardinal
(379) 2 balls;
5th contrast colour (E) purple
(384) 1 ball.
Equivalent yarn: D.K. used
throughout.
1 pair each of 3mm (US 2) and
3¼mm (US 3) knitting needles.
2 spare needles.

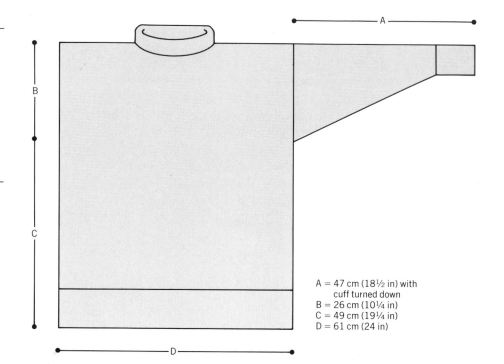

A = 47 cm (18½ in) with
cuff turned down
B = 26 cm (10¼ in)
C = 49 cm (19¼ in)
D = 61 cm (24 in)

One 3mm (US 2) short circular
needle.

TENSION

26 sts and 34 rows to 10cm (4in)
on 3¼mm (US 3) needles over
st st using MC. See page 10.

BACK

With 3mm (US 2) needles and

MC cast on 164 sts and work in
K2, P2, rib for 10cm (4in), inc 1 st
across last row. (165 sts)
Change to 3¼mm (US 3) needles
and starting with a K row work in
st st in MC until back measures
15cm (6in) from cast-on edge,
ending with a ws row.
Place chart
**Next row Keeping in st st,
work across the 55 sts of 1st row of
chart 3 times.
Cont as set until the 40 rows of
chart are worked.
Now work in MC only for a
further 5cm (2in), ending with a
ws row.**
Now work from ** to ** once
more, and then rep the 40 rows of
chart again. (Chart has now been
rep 3 times.)
Now cont straight in MC only
until back measures 75cm
(29½in) from cast-on edge,
ending with a ws row.
Next row Cast off 58 sts, sl
centre 49 sts onto a spare needle,
cast off rem 58 sts.

FRONT

Work as for back until the 3rd rep
of chart has been worked.

TAPESTRY CHART

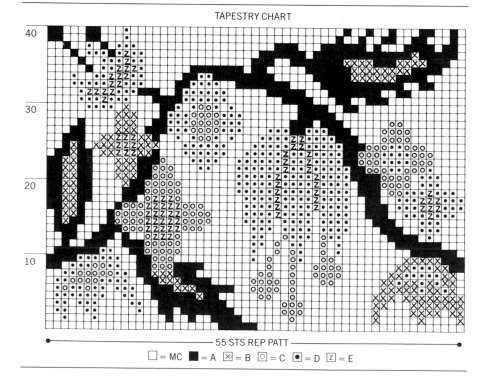

55 STS REP PATT

☐ = MC ■ = A ☒ = B ⊡ = C ⊙ = D ☐ = E

Now cont straight in MC only until front measures 70cm (27½in) from cast-on edge, ending with a ws row.

Shape front neck

Next row K 66 sts, place centre 33 sts onto a spare needle, K across rem 66 sts and work on this last set of sts only.

***Dec 1 st at neck edge on every row until 58 sts rem.

Now cont straight until front measures same as back to cast-off shoulder edge, ending with a ws row. Cast off.

With ws facing rejoin yarn to rem sts and work as for first side from *** to end.

SLEEVES

With 3mm (US 2) needles and MC cast on 68 sts and work in K2, P2, rib for 10cm (4in), inc 2 sts across last row. (70 sts)

Change to 3¼mm (US 3) needles and starting with a K row work in st st in MC, inc 1 st at both ends of every foll 3rd row until there are 138 sts on the needle.

Now cont straight until sleeve measures 47cm (18½in) from cast-on edge, ending with a ws row.

Cast off fairly loosely.

Rep patt for second sleeve.

POLO NECK COLLAR

Join both shoulder seams. With the 3mm (US 2) circular needle and MC and rs facing, pick up and K 21 sts down left front neck, K across centre front sts inc 4 sts across, pick up and K 21 sts up right front neck and finally K across centre back sts inc 4 sts across. (132 sts)

Work in rounds of K2, P2, rib until collar measures 18cm (7in). Cast off loosely ribwise.

TO MAKE UP

With centre of cast-off edges of sleeves to shoulder seams, sew sleeves carefully in position reaching down to same depth on front and back. Join side and sleeve seams, matching patts. Roll collar onto right side and turn cuffs back.

DOUBLE-KNIT ARAN

Traditional Aran knitting wool is almost twice as thick as double-knitting wool, but the raised effects in Aran patterns can look very attractive when worked in lighter yarns, giving a sharper stitch definition. This sweater is fairly simple to knit with its cable and moss stitch pattern. It is a great casual sweater for either men or women and looks good worn with a favourite pair of jeans, as our photograph shows.

MEASUREMENTS

To fit bust/chest
86–91(97–102:107–112)cm
(34–36(38–40:42–44)in).
Actual measurement
126(130:134)cm
(49½(51:52¾)in).
Full length 70cm (27½in).
Sleeve seam 50cm (19¾in).

MATERIALS

Rowan Lightweight D.K. Wool
25g hanks.
Cream (2) 32(32:34) hanks.
Equivalent yarn: D.K.
1 pair each of 2¾mm (US 1) and
3¼mm (US 3) knitting needles.
Cable needle.
2 spare needles.

TENSION

26 sts and 34 rows to 10cm (4in)
on 3¼mm (US 3) needles over
st st. See page 10.

SPECIAL ABBREVIATIONS

C2F = sl next 2 sts onto CN and
leave at front of work, K next 2
sts, then K the 2 sts from CN.
C2B = sl next 2 sts onto CN and
leave at back of work, K next 2 sts
then K the 2 sts from CN.

CABLE PANEL

Worked over 12 sts.
1st row (rs facing) P2, K8, P2.
2nd row K2, P8, K2.
Rep these 2 rows twice more.
7th row P2, C2B, C2F, P2.
8th row As 2nd row.
9th–12th rows As 1st and 2nd
rows.
13th row As 7th row.
14th row As 2nd row.
These 14 rows form the *cable panel*
and are rep as required.

MOSS STITCH PANEL

Worked over 23 sts.
1st row (rs facing) K23.
2nd row P23.
3rd row K11, P1, K11.
4th row P10, K1, P1, K1, P10.

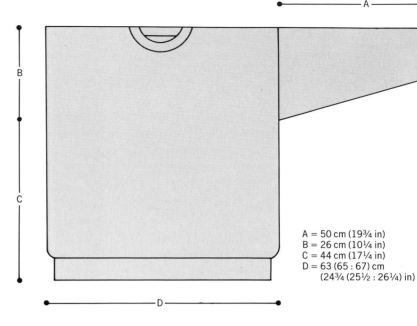

A = 50 cm (19¾ in)
B = 26 cm (10¼ in)
C = 44 cm (17¼ in)
D = 63 (65 : 67) cm
　　(24¾ (25½ : 26¼) in)

5th row K9, (P1, K1) twice, P1,
K9.
6th row P8, (K1, P1) 3 times, K1,
P8.
7th row K7, (P1, K1) 4 times, P1,
K7.
8th row P6, (K1, P1) 5 times, K1,
P6.
9th row K5, (P1, K1) 6 times, P1,
K5.
10th row P4, (K1, P1) 7 times,
K1, P4.
11th row K3, (P1, K1) 8 times,
P1, K3.
12th row P2, (K1, P1) 9 times,
K1, P2.
13th row K23.
14th row P23.
These 14 rows form the *moss stitch
panel* and are rep as required.

BACK

With 2¾mm (US 1) needles cast
on 154(160:166) sts and work in
K1, P1, rib for 6cm (2½in).
Inc row Rib and inc 31 sts evenly
across row. (185(191:197)sts)
Change to 3¼mm (US 3) needles
and place patt as foll:
1st row (rs facing) K22(25:28),
*work across 1st row of *cable panel*,
work across 1st row of *moss stitch
panel*, work across 1st row of *cable

panel, rep from * to last 22(25:28)
sts, k22(25:28).
2nd row P22(25:28), *work
across 2nd row of *cable panel*, work
across 2nd row of *moss stitch panel*,
work across 2nd row of *cable panel*,
rep from * to last 22(25:28) sts,
P22(25:28).
Cont in patts as now set, rep the
14 rows of each panel as required,
and keeping side edges in st st
until 224 patt rows have been
worked (16 complete patts).
Shape back neck
Next row (rs facing) Patt
67(70:73), sl next 51 sts onto a
spare needle, patt to end and work
on this last set of 67(70:73) sts
only.
**Keeping patt correct, dec 1 st at
neck edge on every row until
60(63:66) sts rem.
Cast off.
With ws facing rejoin yarn to rem
sts and work as for first side from
** to end.

FRONT

Work as for back until 194 rows of
patt have been worked, thus
ending with 12th row of 14th patt
rep.
Next row (rs facing) Patt

84(87:90) sts as set, (P1, K1) 8 times, P1, patt 84(87:90) sts as set.

2nd row Patt 83(86:89) sts as set, (K1, P1) 9 times, K1, patt 83(86:89) sts as set.

3rd row Patt 82(85:88) sts as set, (P1, K1) 10 times, P1, patt 82(85:88) sts as set.

4th row Patt 81(84:87) sts as set, (K1, P1) 11 times, K1, patt 81(84:87) sts as set.

5th row Patt 80(83:86) sts as set, (P1, K1) 12 times, P1, patt 80(83:86) sts as set.

6th row Patt 79(82:85) sts as set, (K1, P1) 13 times, K1, patt 79(82:85) sts as set.

7th row Patt 78(81:84) sts as set, (P1, K1) 14 times, P1, patt 78(81:84) sts as set.

8th row Patt 77(80:83) sts as set, (K1, P1) 15 times, K1, patt 77(80:83) sts as set. (202 patt rows now worked.)

Shape front neck

Next row (rs facing) Patt 67(70:73), sl next 51 sts onto a spare needle, patt to end and work on this last set of 67(70:73) sts only.

***Keeping patt correct, dec 1 st at neck edge on every row until 60(63:66) sts rem.

Now cont straight until front measures same as back to cast-off shoulder edge, ending on same patt row.

Cast off.

With ws facing rejoin yarn to rem sts and work as for first side from *** to end.

SLEEVES

With 2¾mm (US 1) needles cast on 78 sts and work in K1, P1, rib for 5cm (2in).

Inc row Rib and inc 16 sts evenly across row. (94 sts)

Change to 3¼mm (US 3) needles and place patt as foll:

1st row (rs facing) *Work across 1st row of *cable panel*, work across 1st row of *moss stitch panel*, work across 1st row of *cable panel*, rep from * once more.

Cont in patts as now set, *at the same time*, inc 1 st at both ends of every foll 6th row until there are 142 sts on the needle, working all inc sts into st st at either side.

Now cont straight until sleeve measures 50cm (19¾in) from cast-on edge, ending with a ws row.

Cast off fairly loosely.

Rep patt for second sleeve.

NECKBAND

Join right shoulder seam carefully matching patts.

With 3¼mm (US 3) needles and rs facing, pick up and K 16 sts down left front neck, K across sts at centre front, pick up and K 16 sts up right front neck, 6 sts down right back neck, K across sts at centre back and finally pick up and K 6 sts up left back neck. (146 sts)

Work in K1, P1, rib for 8 rows.

Cast off fairly loosely ribwise.

TO MAKE UP

Join left shoulder and neckband seam. With centre of cast-off edges of sleeves to shoulder seams, sew sleeves carefully in position, reaching down to same depth on front and back. Join side and sleeve seams.

ETHNIC
FAIR ISLE

T his is my favourite Fair Isle because of the strong, bold pattern and vivid colours. It is difficult to knit though, because the pattern does not repeat at all and there are eleven different colours. It is a classically feminine shape with slightly gathered sleeves, and it also looks good in more muted shades. Like all winter Fair Isles, it is warm to wear because the yarn crossing over at the back gives it a double thickness.

MEASUREMENTS

To fit bust 86(91:97)cm
(34(36:38)in).
Actual measurement
91(97:102)cm (36(38:40)in).
Full length 58cm (23in).
Sleeve seam 47cm (18½in).

MATERIALS

Rowan Silk and Wool 25g balls.
Main colour (MC) black (840)
8(8:9) balls;
1st contrast colour (A) gold (847)
2 balls;
2nd contrast colour (B) red (842)
2 balls;
3rd contrast colour (C) purple
(841) 2 balls;
4th contrast colour (D) royal blue
(848) 2 balls;
5th contrast colour (E) fuchsia
(843) 2 balls;
6th contrast colour (F) yellow
(846) 2 balls.
Rowan Botany 25g hanks.
7th contrast colour (G) ruby (602)
2 hanks;
8th contrast colour (H) pink (621)
2 hanks;
9th contrast colour (I) jade (100)
2 hanks;
10th contrast colour (J) peacock
(633) 2 hanks.
Equivalent yarn: 4-ply used
throughout.
1 pair each of 2¼mm (US 0) and
3¼mm (US 3) knitting needles.
2 spare needles.

TENSION

32 sts and 32 rows to 10cm (4in)
on 3¼mm (US 3) needles over
Fair Isle patt. See page 10.

BACK

With 2¼mm (US 0) needles and
MC cast on 116(120:124) sts and
work in K2, P2, rib for 10cm
(4in).
Inc row Rib and inc 29(35:41) sts
evenly across row. (145(155:165)
sts)
Change to 3¼mm (US 3) needles

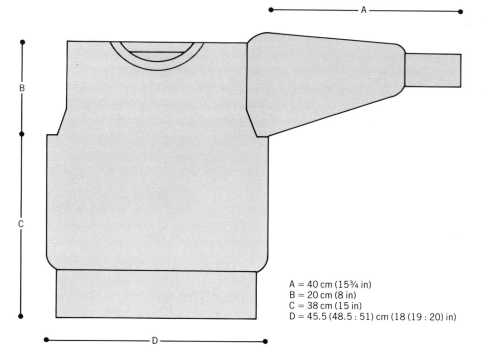

A = 40 cm (15¾ in)
B = 20 cm (8 in)
C = 38 cm (15 in)
D = 45.5 (48.5 : 51) cm (18 (19 : 20) in)

and starting with a K row work in
st st from *back chart* and working
various patt rep as foll:
10 st patt rep Work 2 sts before
dotted line, rep 10 st patt to last
3 sts, work 3 sts beyond dotted
line.
4 st patt rep Work 0(1:0) st
before dotted line, rep the 4 st patt
to last 1(2:1) st(s), work 1(2:1)
st(s) beyond dotted line.
10 st patt rep Work 2 sts before
dotted line, rep 10 st patt to last
3 sts, work 3 sts beyond dotted
line.
2 st patt rep Rep the 2 st patt to
last st, work 1 st beyond dotted
line.
5 st patt rep Rep sts between
dotted lines.
2 st patt rep Rep the 2 st patt to
last st, work 1 st beyond dotted
line.
12 st patt rep Work 0(5:4) sts
before dotted line, rep the 12 st
patt to last 1(6:5) st(s), work
1(6:5) st(s) beyond dotted line.
6 st patt rep Work 0(2:1) st(s)
before dotted line, rep the 6 st
patt to last 1(3:2) st(s), work 1(3:2) sts
beyond dotted line.
Cont working various patt rep as

given until 96th row of chart has
been worked.
Shape armholes
Keeping chart correct and always
centralizing patt.
97th row Cast off 10 sts at beg of
next row in MC.
98th row Cast off 10 sts at beg of
row in B, patt to end.
(125(135:145) sts)
Now keeping chart correct, dec 1
st at both ends of every foll alt row
until 101(111:117) sts rem.
Now cont straight until the 155th
row of chart has been worked,
thus ending with a rs row.
Shape shoulders
With MC, cast off 28(30:32) sts at
beg of next 2 rows.
Leave rem 45(51:53) sts on a
spare needle.

FRONT

Work as for back, shaping
armholes as for back, until 131st
row of chart has been worked,
thus ending with a rs row.
Shape front neck
Next row Patt 37(42:45), turn,
work 2 tog and patt to end of row
and cont on this last set of
36(41:44) sts only.

**Keeping patt correct, dec 1 st at neck edge on every row until 28(30:32) sts rem.
Now cont straight until front measures same as back to cast-off shoulder edge, ending at armhole edge.
Cast off rem 28(30:32) sts in MC.

Return to rem sts and sl centre 27 sts onto a spare needle, with ws facing rejoin yarn to rem sts and patt to end of row.
Next row Patt to last 2 sts, work 2 tog.
Now work as for first side from ** to end.

SLEEVES

With 2¼mm (US 0) needles and MC cast on 68 sts and work in K2, P2, rib for 12cm (4¾in).
Inc row Rib and inc 25 sts evenly across row. (93 sts)
Change to 3¼mm (US 3) needles and starting with a K row work in

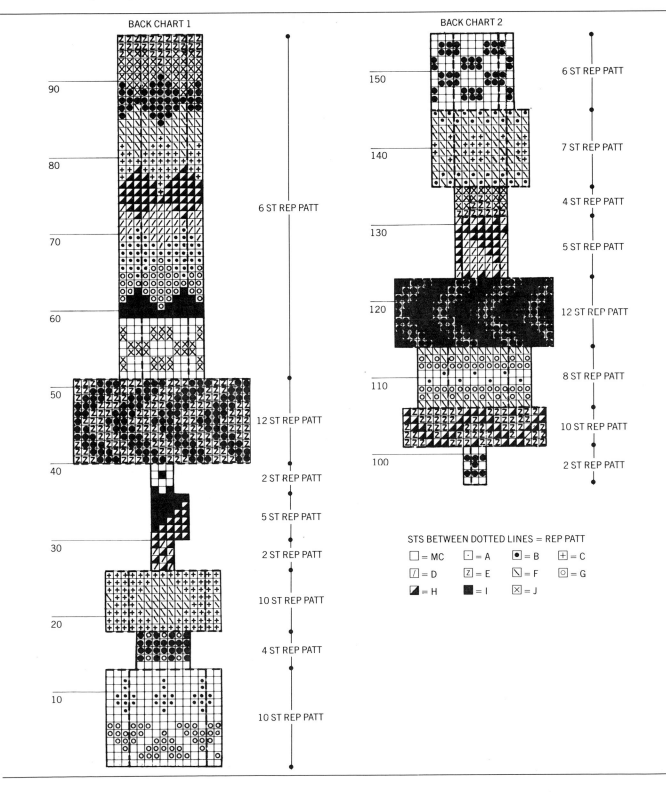

BACK CHART 1

90
80
70
60
50
40
30
20
10

6 ST REP PATT
12 ST REP PATT
2 ST REP PATT
5 ST REP PATT
2 ST REP PATT
10 ST REP PATT
4 ST REP PATT
10 ST REP PATT

BACK CHART 2

150
140
130
120
110
100

6 ST REP PATT
7 ST REP PATT
4 ST REP PATT
5 ST REP PATT
12 ST REP PATT
8 ST REP PATT
10 ST REP PATT
2 ST REP PATT

STS BETWEEN DOTTED LINES = REP PATT

☐ = MC · = A ● = B ⊞ = C
⧄ = D Z = E ⧅ = F ⊙ = G
◣ = H ■ = I ☒ = J

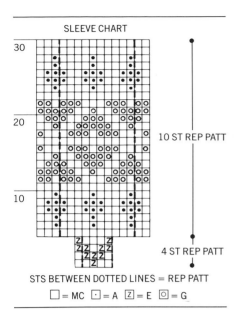

SLEEVE CHART

30

20

10 ST REP PATT

10

4 ST REP PATT

STS BETWEEN DOTTED LINES = REP PATT

□ = MC ⊡ = A ☑ = E ◉ = G

st st from *sleeves chart*, placing chart by rep the 4 st patt to last st, work 1 st beyond dotted line. Cont to work from chart until the 30 rows are complete, *at the same time*, inc 1 st at both ends of every foll 10th row, working inc sts into patt.

Now starting with 15th row of *back chart* cont to foll this chart, inc as set on every foll 10th row until there are 105 sts on the needle, working inc sts into patt.

Now cont straight until 96th row of this chart has been worked. (Same patt row as back/front to beg of armhole shaping.)

Shape top
Cast off 10 sts at beg of next 2 rows.

Keeping chart correct, dec 1 st at both ends of every foll alt row until 69 sts rem.

Work 14 rows straight.

Now dec 1 st at both ends of every foll 4th row until 61 sts rem.

Work 1 row.

Cast off 3 sts at beg of every row until 25 sts rem.

Cast off.

Rep patt for second sleeve.

NECKBAND
Join right shoulder seam.
With 2¼mm (US 0) needles and

MC and rs facing, pick up and K 36(35:36) sts down left front neck, K across centre front sts, pick up and K 36(35:36) sts up right front neck and finally K across centre back sts. (144(148:152) sts)
Work in K2, P2, rib for 7 rows.
Cast off fairly loosely ribwise.

SHOULDER PADS
With 2¼mm (US 0) needles and MC cast on 41 sts and work in single rib as foll:
1st row K1, *P1, K1, rep from * to end.
2nd row P1, *K1, P1, rep from * to end.

Rep last 2 rows, *at the same time*, dec 1 st at both ends of every row until 3 sts rem.
Next row Sl 1, K2 tog, psso. Pull yarn through rem st and secure.
Rep patt for second shoulder pad.

TO MAKE UP
Join left shoulder and neckband seam. Join side and sleeve seams matching patt. Set sleeves into armholes, gathering fullness evenly across top of shoulder. Sew shoulder pads in place. (See note on shoulder pads on page 11.)

JAPANESE SWEATERS

Part of my Japanese collection, these black and cream sweaters were inspired by a beautiful woven scarf that I bought in Japan. The women's sweater has a lovely high, loose neck which is very flattering. The two-colour ribbing at neck and waist is a very strong and unusual way to finish off any sweater. The men's sweater is a simpler, classic shape with a crew neck, knitted with plain ribs, and the children's sweater is a bit shorter and very comfortable to wear.

JAPANESE SWEATER FOR WOMEN

MEASUREMENTS

One size only to fit bust
86–102cm (34–40in).
Actual measurement
114cm (45in).
Full length 71cm (28in).
Sleeve seam 47cm (18½in).

MATERIALS

Rowan Handknit D.K. Cotton
50g balls.
Main colour (MC) ecru (251)
8 balls;
Contrast colour (C) black (252)
7 balls.
Equivalent yarn: D.K.
1 pair each of 4mm (US 5) and
4½mm (US 6) knitting needles.
One 4mm (US 5) short circular
needle.

TENSION

18 sts and 24 rows to 10cm (4in)
on 4½mm (US 6) needles over
st st. See page 10.

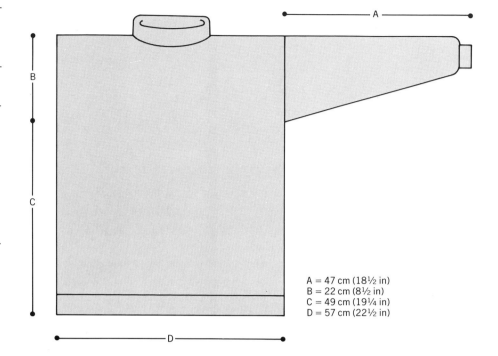

A = 47 cm (18½ in)
B = 22 cm (8½ in)
C = 49 cm (19¼ in)
D = 57 cm (22½ in)

PATTERN 1

Worked over a multiple of 2 sts.
1st row (rs facing) In MC, *K1B,
K1, rep from * to end.
2nd row In MC, K.
3rd row In C, *K1, K1B, rep
from * to end.
4th row In C, K.
These 4 rows form *pattern 1* and
are rep as required.

PATTERN 2

Worked over a multiple of 14 sts
plus 1.
1st row (rs facing) K1MC,
*K13C, K1MC, rep from * to
end.
2nd row P1MC, *P1MC, P11C,
P2MC, rep from * to end.
3rd row K1MC, *K2MC, K9C,
K3MC, rep from * to end.
4th row P1MC, *P3MC, P7C,
P4MC, rep from * to end.
5th row K1MC, *K4MC, K5C,
K5MC, rep from * to end.
6th row P1MC, *P5MC, P3C,
P6MC, rep from * to end.
7th row K1MC, *K6MC, K1C,
K7MC, rep from * to end.
8th row P1C, *P6C, P1MC, P7C,
rep from * to end.
9th row K1C, *K5C, K3MC,
K6C, rep from * to end.
10th row P1C, *P4C, P5MC,
P5C, rep from * to end.
11th row K1C, *K3C, K7MC,
K4C, rep from * to end.
12th row P1C, *P2C, P9MC,
P3C, rep from * to end.
13th row K1C, *K1C, K11MC,
K2C, rep from * to end.
14th row P1C, *P13MC, P1C,
rep from * to end.

These 14 rows form *pattern 2* and are rep as required.

BACK

With 4mm (US 5) needles and C, cast on 112 sts and work in two-tone double rib as foll, carrying yarn not in use loosely across ws:

1st row (rs facing) *K2C, P2MC, rep from * to end.

2nd row *K2MC, P2C, rep from * to end.

Rep these 2 rows until rib measures 5cm (2in), ending with a 2nd row.

K 2 rows in C, thus ending with a ws row.

Now work in *pattern 1* across all sts until 16 rows of this patt have been worked, ending with a ws row and dec 1 st at end of last row only. (111 sts)

Change to 4½mm (US 6) needles and place patt as foll:

1st row (rs facing) K12MC, work 1st row of *pattern 1* across next 8 sts, work 1st row of *pattern 2* across next 71 sts, work 1st row of *pattern 1* across next 8 sts, K12MC.

2nd row P12MC, work 2nd row of *pattern 1* across next 8 sts, work 2nd row of *pattern 2* across next 71 sts, work 2nd row of *pattern 1* across next 8 sts, P12MC.

Cont to rep the relevant patt rows of each patt, keeping both side edges in st st in MC until 112 rows of *pattern 2* have been worked in all (16 rows of triangles complete), thus ending with a ws row.**

Now work in *pattern 1* across all sts, inc 1 st at end of 1st row (112 sts), until 18 rows of this patt have been worked, ending with a ws row.

Next row K12MC, work in *pattern 1* as set across next 8 sts, K72MC, work in *pattern 1* as set across next 8 sts, K12MC.

Next row P12MC, work in *pattern 1* as set across next 8 sts, P72MC, work in *pattern 1* as set across next

8 sts, P12MC.

Keeping centre and side panels in st st in MC and rem in *pattern 1* as set, cont straight for a further 4 rows.

Shape back neck

Next row (rs facing) Patt 42 sts, cast off centre 28 sts, patt to end and work on this last set of 42 sts only.

***Keeping patt correct, dec 1 st at neck edge on next row and foll 5 rows.

Cast off rem 36 sts.

With ws facing rejoin yarn to rem sts and work as for first side from *** to end.

FRONT

Work as for back to **.

Now work in *pattern 1* across all sts, inc 1 st at end of 1st row (112 sts), until 9 rows of this patt have been worked, ending with a rs row.

Shape front neck

Next row Patt 42, cast off centre 28 sts, patt to end and work on this last set of 42 sts only.

Work 1 row.

****Keeping patt correct as for back, cast off 2 sts at beg (neck edge) on next row and foll 2 alt

rows. (36 sts)

Now cont straight, keeping patt correct to match back, until front measures same as back to cast-off shoulder edge, ending with same patt row.

Cast off.

With rs facing rejoin yarn to rem sts and work as for first side from **** to end.

SLEEVES

With 4mm (US 5) needles and MC, cast on 44 sts and work in K2, P2, rib for 8 rows.

Change to 4½mm (US 6) needles and work in *pattern 1* across all sts, rep the 4 row patt throughout, *at the same time*, inc 2 sts at both ends of every foll 12th row until 80 sts are on the needle, working inc sts into the patt.

Now cont straight until sleeve measures 47cm (18½in) from cast-on edge, ending with a ws row.

Cast off.

Rep patt for second sleeve.

TO MAKE UP

Join both shoulder seams matching patts. With centre of cast-off edges of sleeves to shoulder seams, sew sleeves carefully in position, reaching down to same depth on front and back. Join side and sleeve seams.

COLLAR

With the 4mm (US 5) circular needle and MC and rs facing, pick up and K 48 sts around front neck and 32 sts around back neck. (80 sts)

Work in rounds of two-tone double rib as for back welt until collar measures 18cm (7in).

Cast off fairly loosely ribwise.

Fold collar in half to wrong side and sl st loosely in position.

To keep welts in shape, shirring elastic can be added to ribbings at lower edges.

JAPANESE SWEATER FOR MEN

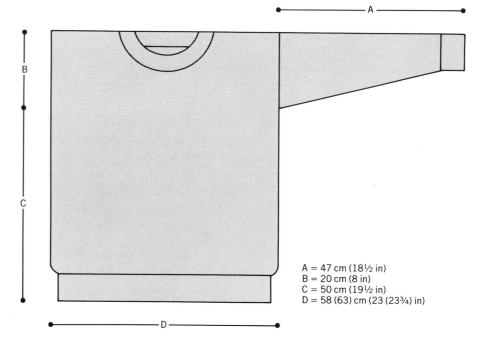

A = 47 cm (18½ in)
B = 20 cm (8 in)
C = 50 cm (19½ in)
D = 58 (63) cm (23 (23¾) in)

MEASUREMENTS

To fit chest 97–102(107–112)cm (38–40(42–44)in).
Actual measurement 116(126)cm (45¾(49¾)in).
Full length 70cm (27½in).
Sleeve seam 47cm (18½).

MATERIALS

Rowan Handknit D.K. Cotton 50g balls.
Main colour (MC) black (252) 14(15) balls;
Contrast colour (C) ecru (251) 11(12) balls.
Equivalent yarn: D.K.
1 pair each of 3¾mm (US 4) and 4½mm (US 6) knitting needles.
One 3¾mm (US 4) short circular needle.

TENSION

18 sts and 22 rows to 10cm (4in) on 4½mm (US 6) needles over Fair Isle patt.
See page 10.

PATTERN 1

Worked over a multiple of 2 sts, using 3¾mm (US 4) needles.

1st row (rs facing) In C, *K1B, K1, rep from * to end.
2nd row In C, K.
3rd row In MC, *K1, K1B, rep from * to end.
4th row In MC, K.
These 4 rows form *pattern 1* and are rep as required.

PATTERN 2

Worked over a multiple of 12 sts, using 4½mm (US 6) needles.
1st row (rs facing) *K6MC, K5C, K1MC, rep from * to end.
2nd row *P2MC, P4C, P6MC, rep from * to end.
3rd row *K1C, K5MC, K4C, K2MC, rep from * to end.
4th row *P3MC, P3C, P4MC, P2C, rep from * to end.
5th row *K2C, K4MC, K2C, K4MC, rep from * to end.
6th row *P4MC, P2C, P3MC, P3C, rep from * to end.
7th row *K4C, K2MC, K1C, K5MC, rep from * to end.
8th row *P8MC, P4C, rep from * to end.
9th row *K5C, K7 MC, rep from * to end.
10th row *P5C, P7MC, rep from * to end.
11th row *K8MC, K4C, rep from * to end.
12th row *P4C, P2MC, P1C, P5MC, rep from * to end.
13th row *K4MC, K2C, K3MC, K3C, rep from * to end.
14th row *P2C, P4MC, P2C, P4MC, rep from * to end.
15th row *K3MC, K3C, K4MC, K2C, rep from * to end.
16th row *P1C, P5MC, P4C, P2MC, rep from * to end.
17th row *K2MC, K4C, K6MC, rep from * to end.
18th row *P6MC, P5C, P1MC,

rep from * to end.
These 18 rows form *pattern 2*.

BACK

With 3¾mm (US 4) needles and
MC, cast on 108(120) sts and
work in K1, P1, rib for 7cm
(2¾in), ending with a ws row.
Now work in *pattern 1* across all sts
until 32 rows of this patt have
been worked, ending with a ws
row.
Change to 4½mm (US 6) needles
and work in *pattern 2* across all sts
until the 18 rows of this patt are
complete.
These 50 rows form one complete
patt.
Note When working *pattern 1* use
3¾mm (US 4) needles, when
working *pattern 2* use 4½mm (US
6) needles.
Cont to rep these 50 rows of patt,
changing needle sizes as
necessary, until 3 reps are worked
(150 rows).
Change to 3¾mm (US 4) needles
and cont in this needle size to
end.**
Now work in *pattern 1* across all sts
for a further 20 rows, thus ending
with a ws row.
Now work in g st (every row K) in
the foll stripe sequence: 2 rows C,
2 rows MC.
Rep these 2 rows until 12 stripe
rows in all have been worked.
Shape back neck
Next row (rs facing) Patt 35(39),
cast off centre 38(42) sts, patt to
end and work on this last set of
35(39) sts only.
***Keeping stripes correct, dec 1
st at neck edge on next 3 rows.
Cast off rem 32(36) sts.
With ws facing rejoin yarn to rem
sts and work as for first side from
*** to end.

FRONT

Work as for back to **.
Now work in *pattern 1* across all sts
for a further 16 rows, thus ending

with a ws row.
Shape front neck
Next row Patt 38(42), cast off
centre 32(36) sts, patt to end and
work on this last set of 38(42) sts
only.
****Dec 1 st at neck edge on next
row and every foll alt row until
32(36) sts rem, changing to the
stripe g st, as for back, on 4th row.
Now cont straight until front
measures same as back to cast-off
shoulder edge, ending on same
patt row.
Cast off.
With ws facing rejoin yarn to rem
sts and work as for first side from
**** to end.

SLEEVES

With 3¾mm (US 4) needles and
MC cast on 36 sts and work in
K1, P1, rib for 10 rows.
Change to 4½mm (US 6) needles
and work in *pattern 1* across all sts,
rep the 4 row patt throughout, *at
the same time*, inc 2 sts at both ends
of every foll 12th row until 72 sts
are on the needle, working inc sts
into the patt.
Now cont straight until sleeve

measures 47cm (18½in) from
cast-on edge ending with a ws
row.
Cast off.
Rep patt for second sleeve.

TO MAKE UP

Join both shoulder seams. With
centre of cast-off edges of sleeves
to shoulder seams, sew sleeves
carefully in position, reaching
down to same depth on front and
back. Join side and sleeve seams
matching patts.

NECKBAND

With the 3¾mm (US 4) circular
needle and MC and rs facing, pick
up and K 12 sts down left front
neck, 30(32) sts from centre front,
12 sts up right front neck, 2 sts
down right back neck, 32(34) sts
from centre back and finally 2 sts
up left back neck. (90(94) sts)
Work in rounds of K1, P1, rib for
14 rounds.
Cast off fairly loosely ribwise.
Fold neckband in half to wrong
side and sl st loosely in position.

JAPANESE SWEATER FOR CHILDREN

MEASUREMENTS
To fit approx age 5–7(8–10) years.
Actual measurement 72(86)cm (28¼(34)in).
Full length 40(48)cm (15¾(19)in).
Sleeve seam 28(36)cm (11(14)in).

MATERIALS
Rowan Handknit D.K. Cotton 50g balls.
Main colour (MC) ecru (251) 6(7) balls;
Contrast colour (C) black (252) 5(6) balls.
Equivalent yarn: D.K.
1 pair each of 3¼mm (US 3) and 4mm (US 5) knitting needles.
Stitch holder.
2 safety pins.
2 spare needles.

TENSION
20 sts and 30 rows to 10cm (4in) on 4mm (US 5) needles over diamond patt.
See page 10.

COLOUR NOTE
When working *diamond pattern* separate balls of yarn *must* be used. Do not strand yarn across ws. See page 10.

MAIN PATTERN
Worked over a multiple of 2 sts.
1st row (rs facing) In C, *K1, K1B, rep from * to end.
2nd row In C, K.
3rd row In MC, *K1B, K1, rep from * to end.
4th row In MC, K.
These 4 rows form the *main pattern* and are rep as required.

DIAMOND PATTERN
Worked over 14 sts.

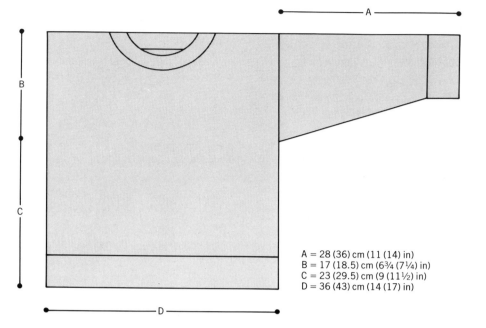

A = 28 (36) cm (11 (14) in)
B = 17 (18.5) cm (6¾ (7¼) in)
C = 23 (29.5) cm (9 (11½) in)
D = 36 (43) cm (14 (17) in)

1st row (rs facing) K6C, K2MC, K6C.
2nd row P6C, P2MC, P6C.
3rd row K5C, K4MC, K5C.
4th row P5C, P4MC, P5C.
5th row K4C, K6MC, K4C.
6th row P4C, P6MC, P4C.
7th row K3C, K8MC, K3C.
8th row P3C, P8MC, P3C.
9th row K2C, K10MC, K2C.
10th row P2C, P10MC, P2C.
11th row K1C, K12MC, K1C.
12th row P1C, P12MC, P1C.
13th row K14MC.
14th row P14MC.
15th row As 11th row.
16th row As 12th row.
17th row As 9th row.
18th row As 10th row.
19th row As 7th row.
20th row As 8th row.
21st row As 5th row.
22nd row As 6th row.
23rd row As 3rd row.
24th row As 4th row.
These 24 rows form the *diamond pattern* and are rep as required.

BACK
With 3¼mm (US 3) needles and MC, cast on 72(84) sts and work in K2, P2, rib for 5cm (2in), inc 0(2) sts evenly across

last row. (72(86) sts)
Change to 4mm (US 5) needles and divide back as foll:
1st row (rs facing) Work first 10(16) sts as 1st row of *main pattern*, turn, and work on this first set of sts only, leaving rem sts on a st holder.
Keeping main patt correct, cont straight on these 10(16) sts until this section measures 40(48)cm (15¾(19)in) from cast-on edge ending with a ws row. Cast off.
Return to rem sts on st holder and sl first 14 sts onto a safety pin, with rs facing rejoin yarn to rem sts and work across next 24(26) sts as 1st row of *main pattern*, turn, and work on this first set of sts only, leaving rem sts on st holder. Keeping main correct, cont straight on these 24(26) sts until this section measures same as first section ending with a ws row and same patt row.
Next row Cast off 3 sts, sl next 18(20) sts onto a spare needle, cast off rem 3 sts.
Return to rem sts on st holder and sl first 14 sts onto a safety pin, with rs facing rejoin yarn to rem sts and work across these 10(16) sts as 1st row of *main pattern*, turn.

Now work as for first side from ** to **.

With rs facing rejoin yarn to one set of sts on safety pin and work across these sts as 1st row of *diamond pattern*, rep rows as required, until this section, when slightly stretched, measures same as side sections to cast-off shoulder edge. Cast off. Work across other sts on second safety pin in same manner.

Now using a flat st carefully join sections together.

FRONT

Cast on and work rib as for back welt. Cont as for back, working both side sections in *main pattern*

and both *diamond patterns* as for back.

Work centre section as foll:
With rs facing rejoin yarn to centre 24(26) sts and work in *main pattern* as for back until this section measures 35(42)cm (13¾(16½)in) from cast-on edge, ending with a ws row.

Shape front neck

Next row Patt 8 sts, turn, work 2 tog and patt to end of row and cont on this last set of 7 sts only.
***Keeping patt correct, dec 1 st at neck edge on every row until 3 sts rem.

Cont straight on these sts until this section measures same as side sections, ending with a ws row

and same patt row. Cast off.
Return to rem sts and sl next 8(10) sts onto a spare needle, with rs facing rejoin yarn to rem sts and patt to end of row.

Next row Patt to last 2 sts, work 2 tog.

Now work as for first side from *** to end.

Join sections together as for back.

SLEEVES

With 3¼mm (US 3) needles and MC, cast on 32(36) sts and work in K2, P2, rib for 5cm (2in), inc 0(2) sts evenly across last row. (32(38) sts)

Change to 4mm (US 5) needles and work in *main pattern, at the same time*, inc 2 sts at both ends of every foll 6th(8th) row until there are 68(74) sts on the needle, working inc sts into the patt.

Now cont straight until sleeve measures 28(36)cm (11(14)in) from cast-on edge, ending with a ws row.

Cast off fairly loosely.
Rep patt for second sleeve.

NECKBAND

Join right shoulder seam.
With 3¼mm (US 3) needles and MC, and rs facing, pick up and K 16(20) sts down left front neck, K across centre front sts, pick up and K 16(20) sts up right front neck and finally K across centre back sts, inc 2 sts across. (60(72) sts)

Work in K2, P2, rib for 2.5cm (1in).

Cast off loosely ribwise.

TO MAKE UP

Join left shoulder and neckband seam. With centre of cast-off edges of sleeves to shoulder seams, sew sleeves carefully in position reaching down to same depth on front and back. Join side and sleeve seams.

PEOPLE CARDIGAN
AND SWEATER

This can be made as a round-necked cardigan for women or a sweater with a collar for little girls. It is based on the embroidered samplers that young girls used to make in the Victorian era to show off their needlework. They would work different shapes and patterns to demonstrate all the stitches they could do. My sweater has flowers, people, and shamrocks, and I think it looks best in bright colours.

PEOPLE CARDIGAN

MEASUREMENTS
To fit bust 86–91(97–102)cm (32–36(38–40)in).
Actual measurement 106(112)cm (41¾(44)in).
Full length 68(70)cm (26¾(27½)in).
Sleeve seam 48cm (19in).

MATERIALS
Rowan Lightweight D.K. Wool 25g hanks.
Main colour (MC) red (115) 20(22) hanks;
1st contrast colour (A) yellow (12) 2 hanks;
2nd contrast colour (B) royal blue (56) 2 hanks;
3rd contrast colour (C) navy (97) 3 hanks;
4th contrast colour (D) emerald (124) 3 hanks;
5th contrast colour (E) purple (126) 1 hank;
6th contrast colour (F) fuchsia (96) 1 hank;
7th contrast colour (G) orange (510) 1 hank.
Equivalent yarn: D.K.
1 pair each of 2¾mm (US 1) and 3¼mm (US 3) knitting needles.
13 buttons.
3 spare needles.

TENSION
28 sts and 34 rows to 10cm (4in) on 3¼mm (US 3) needles over patt. See page 10.

BACK
With 2¾mm (US 1) needles and MC, cast on 152(160) sts and work in K2, P2, rib for 5cm (2in), on last row inc 1 st. (153(161) sts) Change to 3¼mm (US 3) needles and starting with a K row work in st st from chart as foll:
1st row (rs facing) Work 6(0) sts before the dotted line, now rep the

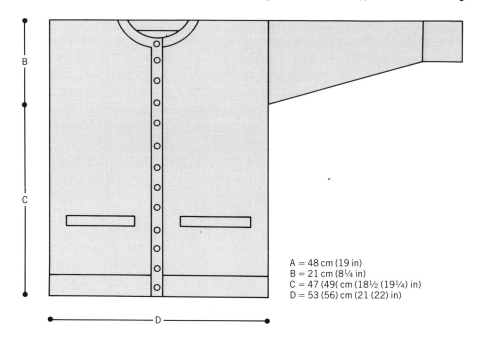

A = 48 cm (19 in)
B = 21 cm (8¼ in)
C = 47 (49(cm (18½ (19¼) in)
D = 53 (56) cm (21 (22) in)

20 st patt 7(8) times across row, work 7(1) st(s) beyond the dotted line.
2nd row Work 7(1) st(s) before the dotted line, rep the 20 st patt 7(8) times across row, work 6(0) sts beyond the dotted line. The chart is now set. Cont working from chart, rep the 102 rows twice, and noting the rows that are to be worked only as K rows. (204 patt rows worked.)
Now cont straight in st st in MC only until back measures 68(70)cm (26¾(27½) in) from cast-on edge, ending with a ws row.
Shape shoulders
With MC only, cast off 50(52) sts at beg of next 2 rows.
Leave rem 53(57) sts on a spare needle.

POCKET LININGS
With 3¼mm (US 3) needles and MC, cast on 47 sts and starting with a K row work in st st for 40 rows, thus ending with a ws row.
Leave sts on a spare needle.
Rep patt for second pocket lining.

RIGHT FRONT
With 2¾mm (US 3) needles and MC, cast on 76(80) sts and work in K2, P2, rib for 5cm (2in), on last row inc 1 st. (77(81) sts) Change to 3¼mm (US 3) needles and starting with a K row work in st st from chart as foll:
1st row (rs facing) Work 19(1) st(s) before the dotted line, now rep the 20 st patt 2(4) times across row, work 18(0) sts beyond the dotted line.
The chart is now set. Cont working from chart until 40 rows have been worked.
Place pocket
Next row (41st row of chart) Patt 15(17), place next 47 sts on a spare needle and in their place patt across the 47 sts from first pocket lining, patt to end of row. Now cont across all 77(81) sts until front measures 60(62)cm (23½(24½)in) from cast-on edge, ending at centre front edge.
Shape front neck
Cast off 12 sts at beg (neck edge) of next row.
Keeping patt correct, dec 1 st at neck edge on every row until 50(52) sts rem.

Now cont straight until front measures same as back to cast-off shoulder edge, ending at side edge. Cast off.

LEFT FRONT

Work as for right front, reversing front neck shaping.

SLEEVES

With 2¾mm (US 1) needles and MC, cast on 60 sts and work in K2, P2, rib for 10cm (4in).

Inc row Rib and inc 21 sts evenly across row. (81 sts)
Change to 3¼mm (US 3) needles

and starting with a K row work in st st from chart, starting from 81st row as foll:

81st row (rs facing) Work 0 sts before the dotted line, rep the 20 st patt 4 times across row, work 1 st beyond the dotted line. The chart is now set. Cont to follow chart, *at the same time*, inc 1 st at both ends of every foll 6th row until there are 121 sts on the needle.

Note Work all inc sts into the small patts, but work only *complete 'people' motifs*.
Cont as set until 124 patt rows have been worked.
Now cont straight in st st in MC until sleeve measures 48cm (19in) from cast-on edge, ending with a ws row.
Cast off loosely.
Rep patt for second sleeve.

BUTTON BAND

With 2¾mm (US 1) needles and MC and rs facing, pick up and K 192(196) sts down left front edge.
Work in K2, P2, rib for 7 rows.
Cast off loosely ribwise.

BUTTONHOLE BAND

With 2¾mm (US 1) needles and MC and rs facing, pick up and K 192(196) sts up right front edge.
Work in P2, K2, rib for 3 rows.
Buttonhole row (rs facing) Rib 4(6), *cast off 2 sts, rib 14, rep from * to last 12(14) sts, cast off 2 sts, rib to end.
Next row Rib casting on 2 sts over cast-off sts on previous row. (12 buttonholes worked.)
Work 2 more rows in rib.
Cast off loosely ribwise.

NECKBAND

Join both shoulder seams.
With 2¾mm (US 1) needles and rs facing and MC, pick up and K 40 sts up right front neck including top of buttonhole band,

CARDIGAN AND SWEATER CHART

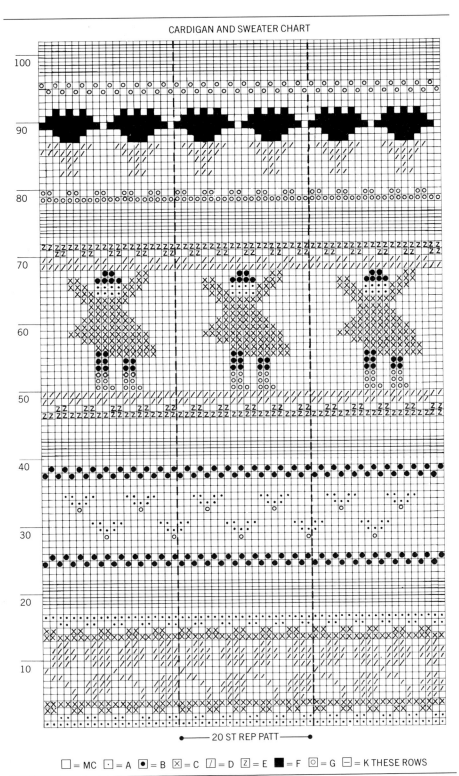

←———— 20 ST REP PATT ————→

☐ = MC ⊡ = A ◉ = B ⊠ = C ⊘ = D ☒ = E ■ = F ⊙ = G ⊟ = K THESE ROWS

K across sts at back neck, then pick up and K 39 sts down left front neck including top of button band. (132(136) sts)

Work in K2, P2, rib for 3 rows.

Buttonhole row (rs facing) Rib 4, cast off 2 sts, rib to end.

Next row Rib, casting on 2 sts over cast-off sts on previous row. Rib 2 more rows.

Cast off loosely ribwise.

POCKET TOPS

With 2¾mm (US 1) needles and MC and rs facing, work in K2, P2, rib across the 47 sts of one pocket top, inc 1 st on first row. (48 sts) Work 7 rows in rib.

Cast off loosely ribwise.

TO MAKE UP

With centre of cast-off edges of sleeves to shoulder seams, sew sleeves carefully in position reaching down to same patt row on front and back. Join side and sleeve seams. Catch down side edges of pocket tops and sl st pocket linings neatly in position on wrong side. Sew on buttons to correspond with buttonholes.

PEOPLE SWEATER

MEASUREMENTS

To fit approx age 7–8(9:10–11:12) years. Actual measurement 74(80:85:91)cm (29(31½:33½:36)in). Full length 50(54:58:60)cm (19¾(21¼:23:23¾)in). Sleeve seam approx 30(38:38:43)cm (12(15:15:17)in).

MATERIALS

Rowan Lightweight D.K. Wool 25g hanks.

Main colour (MC) navy (97) 15(15:16:16) hanks;

1st contrast colour (A) yellow (12) 1(1:1:1) hank;

2nd contrast colour (B) red (44) 1(1:2:2) hank(s);

3rd contrast colour (C) emerald (124) 2(2:3:3) hanks;

4th contrast colour (D) royal blue (56) 1(1:1:1) hank;

5th contrast colour (E) purple (126) 1(1:1:1) hank;

6th contrast colour (F) fuchsia (96) 1(1:1:1) hank;

7th contrast colour (G) orange (510) 1(1:1:1) hank.

Equivalent yarn: D.K.

1 pair each of 3mm (US 2) and 3¼mm (US 3) knitting needles.

4 spare needles.

One 3mm (US 2) short circular needle.

TENSION

28 sts and 34 rows to 10cm (4in) on 3¼mm (US 3) needles over patt.

See page 10.

CHART NOTE

The chart for this patt is the same as the chart for the People Cardigan (see page 127).

BACK

With 3mm (US 2) needles and MC, cast on 103(111:119:127) sts and work in K1, P1, rib for 6cm (2½in).

Change to 3¼mm (US 3) needles and starting with a K row work in st st from chart and starting on appropriate patt row as foll:

45th(45th:1st:1st) row (rs facing) Work 2(6:10:4) sts before the dotted line, now rep the 20 st patt 5(5:5:6) times across row, work 1(5:9:3) st(s) beyond the dotted line.

46th(46th:2nd:2nd) row Work 1(5:9:3) st(s) before the dotted line, rep the 20 st patt 5(5:5:6) times across row, work 2(6:10:4) sts beyond the dotted line.

The chart is now set. Cont working from chart, rep the 102 rows as required, and noting the rows that are to be worked only as K rows, also only 'complete' people motifs should be worked, working other sts in MC.

Cont as set until back measures 50(54:58:60)cm (19¾(21¼: 23:23¾)in) from cast-on edge

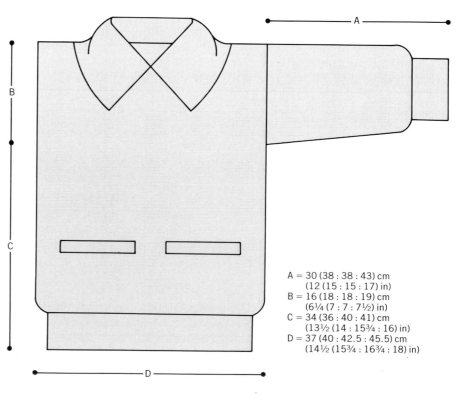

A = 30 (38 : 38 : 43) cm
    (12 (15 : 15 : 17) in)
B = 16 (18 : 18 : 19) cm
    (6¼ (7 : 7 : 7½) in)
C = 34 (36 : 40 : 41) cm
    (13½ (14 : 15¾ : 16) in)
D = 37 (40 : 42.5 : 45.5) cm
    (14½ (15¾ : 16¾ : 18) in)

ending with a ws row.
Shape shoulders
Keeping patt correct cast off 34(37:40:43) sts at beg of next 2 rows.
Leave rem 35(37:39:41) sts on a spare needle.

POCKET LININGS
With 3¼mm (US 3) needles and MC, cast on 34 sts and starting with a K row work in st st for 36 rows, thus ending with a ws row.
Leave sts on a spare needle.
Rep patt for second pocket lining.

FRONT
Work as for back until 36 rows of patt have been worked, thus ending with a ws row.
Place pockets
Next row Patt 7(9:12:14), *place

next 34 sts on a spare needle and in their place patt across the 34 sts of first pocket lining*, patt next 21(25:27:31) sts, then rep from * to * once more working across sts of second pocket lining, patt to end of row.
Cont in patt as set across all sts until front measures 46(50:53:55)cm (18(19¾:21: 21¾)in) from cast-on edge, ending with a ws row.
Shape front neck
Next row Patt 42(45:48:51), turn, work 2 tog, patt to end of row and cont on this last set of 41(44:47:50) sts only.
**Keeping patt correct dec 1 st at neck edge on every row until 34(37:40:43) sts rem. Now cont straight until front measures same as back to cast-off shoulder edge, ending at side edge. Cast off.
Return to rem sts and slip centre 19(21:23:25) sts on a spare needle, with rs facing rejoin yarn to rem sts and patt to end of row.
Next row Work to last 2 sts, work 2 tog.
Now work as for first side from ** to end.

SLEEVES
With 3mm (US 2) needles and MC cast on 54 sts and work in K1, P1, rib for 6cm (2½in).
Inc row Rib and inc 13 sts evenly across row. (67 sts)
Change to 3¼mm (US 3) needles and starting with a K row work in st st from chart and starting on appropriate patt row as foll:
43rd(19th:19th:1st) row (rs facing) Work 4 sts before the dotted line, now rep the 20 st patt 3 times across row, work 3 sts beyond the dotted line.
44th(20th:20th:2nd) row Work 3 sts before the dotted line, now rep the 20 st patt 3 times across row, work 2 sts beyond the dotted line.
The chart is now set. Cont to foll

chart, *at the same time*, inc 1 st at both ends of every foll 6th row until there are 91(101:101:105) sts on the needle. (*Note* work all inc sts into the small patts, but work only complete 'people' motifs.)
Now cont straight until sleeve measures approx 30(38:38:43)cm (12(15:15:17)in) from cast-on edge, ending with a ws row and only when a complete motif has been worked.
Cast off fairly loosely.
Rep patt for second sleeve.

COLLAR
Join both shoulder seams.
With the 3mm (US 2) circular needle and MC and rs facing, pick up and K 19(19:22:22) sts down left front neck, K across centre front sts, pick up and K 19(19:22:22) sts up right front neck and finally K across centre back sts. (92(96:104:110) sts)
Work in rounds of K1, P1, rib for 6 rounds, ending at centre front.
Divide for collar
Next row Rib to centre front, turn, and work backwards and forwards in rows of K1, P1, rib until collar measures 8cm (3in) from division.
Cast off loosely ribwise.

POCKET TOPS
With 3mm (US 2) needles and MC and rs facing, work across one set of sts on spare needle in K1, P1, rib for 6 rows.
Cast off fairly loosely ribwise.

TO MAKE UP
With centre of cast-off edges of sleeves to shoulder seams, sew sleeves carefully in position reaching down to same depth on front and back. Join side and sleeve seams. Catch down side edges of pocket tops and sl st pocket linings neatly in position on wrong side. Turn collar over to right side.

BLACK AND CREAM FITTED CARDIGAN

The black and cream ribbing is what makes this sweater, from my Japanese collection, so attractive and unusual. The gathering at the waist could be accentuated very effectively with a big black belt. This is one of the few sweaters I have designed with a zip rather than buttons, making it more like a jacket. It could be dressed up for evening wear with a short black skirt and lots of jewellery.

MEASUREMENTS

To fit bust
81–86(91–97:102–107)cm
(32–34(36–38:40–42)in).
Actual measurement
108(117:126)cm
(42½(46:49½)in).
Full length 70cm (27½in).
Sleeve seam 47cm (18½in).

MATERIALS

Rowan Handknit D.K. Cotton
50g balls.
Main colour (MC) black (252)
16(18:20) balls;
Contrast colour (C) ecru (251)
14(16:18) balls.
Equivalent yarn: D.K.
1 pair each of 3mm (US 2) and
3¾mm (US 4) knitting needles.
65cm (26in) heavy black
open-ended plastic zip fastener.
2 spare needles.

TENSION

18 sts and 28 rows to 10cm (4in)
on 3¾mm (US 4) needles over
patt. See page 10.

BACK

With 3mm (US 2) needles and
MC, cast on 96(104:112) sts and
work in two-tone double rib as
foll, carrying yarn not in use
loosely across ws:
1st row (rs facing) *K2MC, P2C,
rep from * to end.
2nd row *K2C, P2MC, rep from
* to end.
Rep these 2 rows until rib
measures 5cm (2in), ending with
a 2nd row.
Change to 3¾mm (US 4) needles
and work in patt as foll:
1st row (rs facing) In MC, *K1B,
K1, rep from * to end.
2nd row In MC, K.
3rd row In C, *K1, K1B, rep
from * to end.
4th row In C, K.
These 4 rows form the patt and
are rep as required. Cont in patt
as set until back measures approx

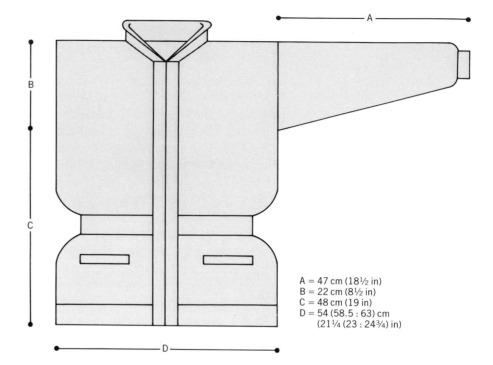

A = 47 cm (18½ in)
B = 22 cm (8½ in)
C = 48 cm (19 in)
D = 54 (58.5 : 63) cm
(21¼ (23 : 24¾) in)

22cm (8¾in) from cast-on edge,
ending with a 4th patt row.
Dec row (rs facing) With MC, K
and dec 36 sts evenly across row.
(60(68:76) sts)
Change to 3mm (US 2) needles
and starting with a 2nd row, work
in two-tone double rib as for welt
for 5cm (2in) ending with a rs row.
Inc row With MC, K and inc 36
sts evenly across row.
(96(104:112) sts)
Change to 3¾mm (US 4) needles
and work in patt as before until
back measures 68cm (26¾in)
from cast-on edge, ending with a
ws row.
Shape back neck
Next row Patt 38(42:46), cast off
centre 20 sts, patt to end and work
on this last set of 38(42:46) sts
only.
Work 1 row.
**Keeping patt correct, cast off 2
sts at beg (neck edge) on next row
and every foll alt row until
32(36:40) sts rem.
Cast off.
With ws facing rejoin yarn to rem
sts and work as for first side
from ** to end.

POCKET LININGS

With 3¾mm (US 4) needles and
MC cast on 24 sts and starting
with a K row work in st st for
10cm (4in), ending with a
ws row.
Leave sts on a spare needle.
Rep patt for second pocket
lining.

RIGHT FRONT

With 3mm (US 2) needles and
MC, cast on 44(48:52) sts and
work in two-tone double rib as for
back welt for 5cm (2in), ending
with a 2nd row.
Change to 3¾mm (US 4) needles
and work in patt as for back until
front measures 15cm (6in) from
cast-on edge, ending with a ws
row.
Place pocket
Next row Patt 10(12:14), sl next
24 sts onto a spare needle and in
their place patt across the 24 sts of
first pocket lining, patt rem
10(12:14) sts.
Cont in patt across sts until front
measures approx 22cm (8¾in)
from cast-on edge, ending with a
4th patt row.

Dec row (rs facing) With MC, K and dec 16 sts evenly across row. (28(32:36) sts)
Change to 3mm (US 2) needles and starting with a 2nd row work in two-tone double rib as for welt for 5cm (2in) ending with a rs row.
Inc row With MC, K and inc 16 sts evenly across row. (44(48:52) sts)
Change to 3¾mm (US 4) needles and work in patt as before until front measures 63cm (25in) from cast-on edge, ending with a ws row.
Shape front neck
Keeping patt correct, cast off 2 sts at beg (neck edge) on next row and every foll alt row until 32(36:40) sts rem.
Now work straight until front measures same as back to cast-off shoulder edge, ending on same patt row.
Cast off.

LEFT FRONT

Work as for right front reversing front neck shaping.

SLEEVES

With 3mm (US 2) needles and MC cast on 44 sts and work in two-tone double rib as for back welt for 3cm (1¼in), ending with a 2nd row.
Change to 3¾mm (US 4) needles and work in patt as for back, rep the 4 row patt throughout, *at the same time*, inc 2 sts at both ends of every foll 12th row until 80 sts are on the needle, working inc sts into the patt.
Now cont straight until sleeve measures 47cm (18½in) from cast-on edge, ending with a ws row.
Cast off.
Rep patt for second sleeve.

TO MAKE UP

Join both shoulder seams. With centre of cast-off edges of sleeves to shoulder seams, sew sleeves carefully in position, reaching down to same depth on front and back. Join side and sleeve seams matching ribs.

POCKET TOPS

With 3mm (US 2) needles and rs facing work in two-tone double rib across the 24 sts, as for back welt, for 3cm (1¼in).
Cast off loosely ribwise in colours as set.
St pocket tops down at each side and st linings neatly in position on wrong side.

FRONT BANDS

With 3mm (US 2) needles and MC, pick up and K 148 sts evenly across one front edge.
Work in two-tone double rib as for back welt for 3cm (1¼in).
Cast off loosely ribwise in colours as set.

Note When working 2nd band, reverse colours of two-tone rib so as stripes will match exactly at centre front.

COLLAR

With 3¾mm (US 4) needles and MC cast on 84 sts.
Starting with a K row, work in st st for 3cm (1¼in), ending with a ws row.
Change to 3mm (US 2) needles and work in two-tone double rib for 6 rows.
Now dec 2 sts at each end of *every* row until 36 sts rem, keeping rib patt correct.
Cast off fairly loosely ribwise in colours as set.
Sew cast-off edge of collar to neck edge, starting and finishing at edge of front bands, and allowing st st top of collar to roll over onto rs. Sew zip neatly in position down front edges of cardigan.

ANIMAL
SWEATER

I was inspired to design this range, which includes sweaters for grown-ups too, after visiting the 'Oh India' exhibition at the Metropolitan Museum in New York. There was a wonderful silk tapestry wall-hanging there, covered in exotic animals such as lions, tigers and monkeys. I chose different animals for my sweaters – the adult version has a horse, a spider and a butterfly – and used bright colours rather than the muted Indian shades.

MEASUREMENTS

To fit approx age 5–6 (7–8: 9–10) years.
Actual measurement 70(80:90)cm (27½(31½:35½)in).
Full length 36(39.5:43)cm (14¼(15½:17)in).
Sleeve seam 26(27.5:29)cm (10¼(10¾:11½)in).

MATERIALS

Rowan Handknit D.K. Cotton 50g balls.
Main colour (MC) either black (252) or ecru (251) 6(7:7) balls;
1st contrast colour (A) either sunflower (261) or black (252) 2(2:2) balls;
2nd contrast colour (B) either hastings green (281) or cherry (298) 1(1:1) ball;
3rd contrast colour (C) either cherry (298) or hastings green (281) 1(1:1) ball.
Equivalent yarn: D.K.
1 pair each of 3¾mm (US 4) and 4mm (US 5) knitting needles.
One 3¾mm (US 4) short circular needle.

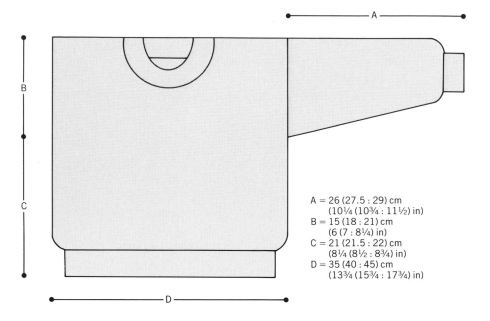

A = 26 (27.5 : 29) cm
 (10¼ (10¾ : 11½) in)
B = 15 (18 : 21) cm
 (6 (7 : 8¼) in)
C = 21 (21.5 : 22) cm
 (8¼ (8½ : 8¾) in)
D = 35 (40 : 45) cm
 (13¾ (15¾ : 17¾) in)

TENSION

20 sts and 28 rows to 10cm (4in) on 4mm (US 5) needles over st st. See page 10.

BACK

With 3¾mm (US 4) needles and MC, cast on 64(72:80) sts and work in two-tone double rib as foll, carrying yarn not in use loosely across ws:

1st row (rs facing) *K2A, P2MC, rep from * to end.
2nd row *K2MC, P2A, rep from * to end.
Rep these 2 rows until rib measures 4cm (1½in), ending with a 1st row.
Inc row (ws facing) With MC, P and inc 6(8:10) sts evenly across

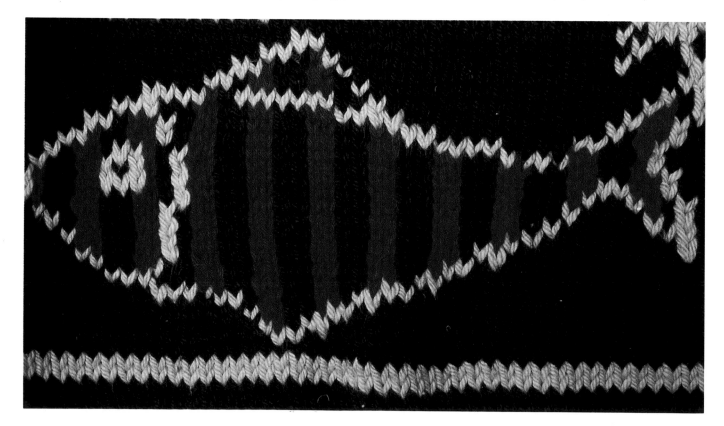

BACK AND FRONT CHART

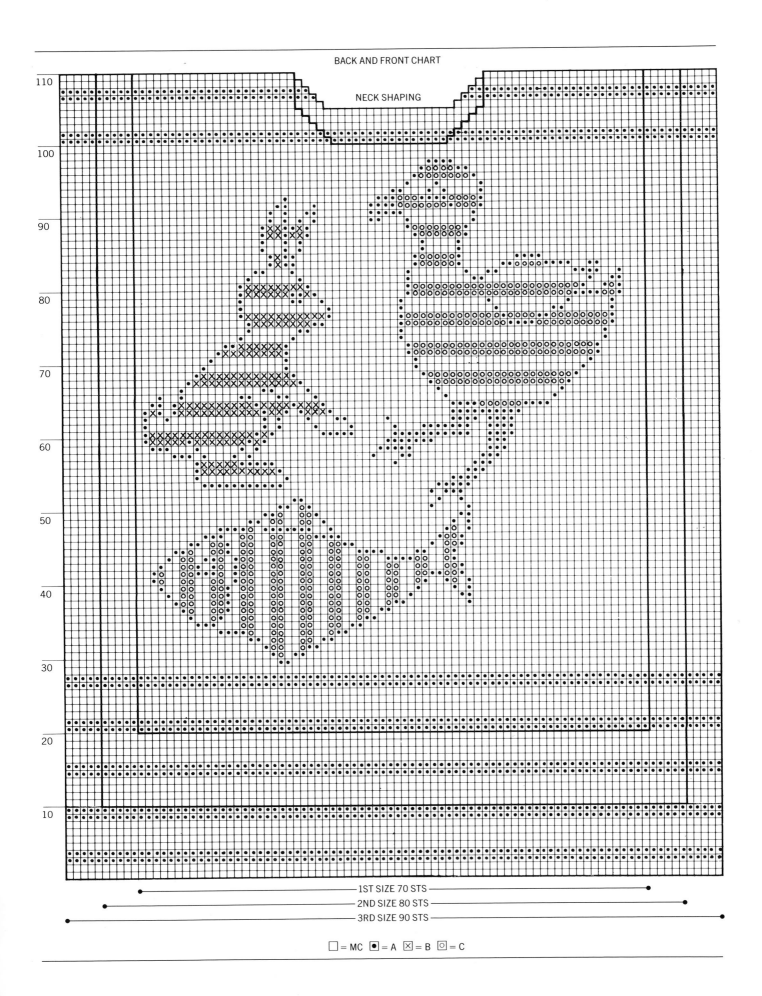

NECK SHAPING

1ST SIZE 70 STS
2ND SIZE 80 STS
3RD SIZE 90 STS

□ = MC   ⊡ = A   ⊠ = B   ⊙ = C

row. (70(80:90) sts)
Change to 4mm (US 5) needles and starting with a K row work in st st from *back chart*, starting on 21st(11th:1st) row and working between appropriate lines for size required.
Cont straight until 105th row of chart has been worked.
Shape back neck
Next row (ws facing – 106th row of chart) Patt 26(31:36), cast off centre 18 sts, patt to end and cont on this last set of 26(31:36) sts only.
**Keeping patt correct, dec 1 st

at neck edge on every row until 22(27:32) sts rem, ending on 110th row of chart.
Cast off.
With rs facing rejoin yarn to rem sts and work as for first side from ** to end.

FRONT
Work as for back until 100th row of chart has been worked.
Shape front neck
Next row (rs facing – 101st row of chart) Patt 27(32:37), cast off centre 16 sts, patt to end and cont on this last set of

27(32:37) sts only.
***Keeping patt correct, dec 1 st at neck edge on every row until 22(27:32) sts rem.
Now cont straight until front measures same as back to cast-off shoulder edge.
Cast off.
With ws facing rejoin yarn to rem sts and work as for first side from *** to end.

FIRST SLEEVE
With 3¾mm (US 4) needles and MC, cast on 32(36:40) sts and work in two-tone double rib as for

SLEEVE CHART

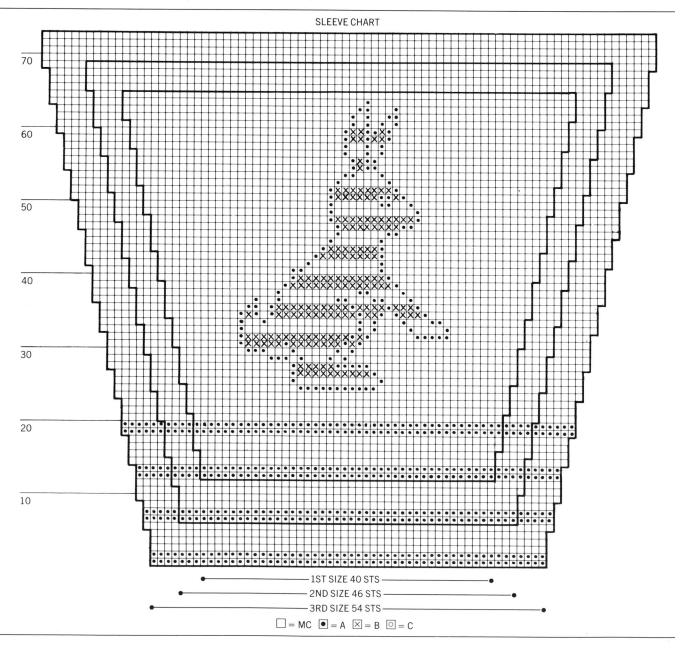

70
60
50
40
30
20
10

•———— 1ST SIZE 40 STS ————•
•———— 2ND SIZE 46 STS ————•
•———— 3RD SIZE 54 STS ————•

☐ = MC   ⊡ = A   ⊠ = B   ⊙ = C

back welt for 3cm (1¼in), ending with a 1st row.
Inc row (ws facing) With MC, P and inc 8(10:14) sts evenly across row. (40(46:54) sts)
Change to 4mm (US 5) needles and starting with a K row work in st st from *sleeve chart*, starting on 13th(7th:1st) row working and between appropriate lines for size required, *at the same time*, inc 1 st at both ends of rows as indicated on chart until there are 62(72:84) sts on the needle.
Now cont straight until

65th(69th:73rd) row of chart is complete.
Cast off fairly loosely in MC.

SECOND SLEEVE
Work as for first sleeve working the stripes but omit the rabbit motif.

NECKBAND
Join both shoulder seams.
With the 3¾mm (US 4) circular needle and rs facing and MC, pick up and K 38 sts from around front neck and 30 sts from around back

neck. (68 sts)
Work in rounds of K2, P2, rib for 3cm (1¼in).
Cast off loosely ribwise.

TO MAKE UP
With centre of cast-off edges of sleeves to shoulder seams, sew sleeves carefully in position reaching down to same depth on front and back. Join side and sleeve seams matching stripes.
To keep welts in shape, shirring elastic can be added to ribbings at lower edges.

FITTED SWEATER IN SILK

This is one of our most popular styles and one of my personal favourites, as it is extremely flattering to wear. The fitted waist could be accentuated even more with a wide belt. It is basically an evening style, and is also good for wearing under a suit for a smart day-time outfit or restaurant-wear. It looks good knitted in wool or cotton, but silk gives the most luxurious effect.

MEASUREMENTS

To fit bust 86(91:97)cm
(34(36:38)in).
Actual measurement
91(97:102)cm (36(38:40)in).
Full length 52(52:55)cm
(20½(20½:21¾)in).
Sleeve seam 45cm (17¾in).

MATERIALS

Rowan Mulberry Silk 50g hanks.
Peony (877) 9(9:10) hanks.
Equivalent yarn: 4-ply.
1 pair each of 2mm (US 00) and
3mm (US 2) knitting needles.
Cable needle.
1 button.

TENSION

28 sts and 36 rows to 10cm (4in)
on 3mm (US 2) needles over st st.
See page 10.

SPECIAL ABBREVIATIONS

M1 = make 1 by picking up loop
that lies between st just worked
and foll st and working into back
of it.
Cr3B = sl next 3 sts onto CN and
leave at back of work, K2, P1,
now P1, K2 across sts on CN.
Cr3F = sl next 3 sts onto CN and
leave at front of work, K2, P1,
now P1, K2 across sts on CN.
C2B = sl next 2 sts onto CN and
leave at back of work, K2, then
K2 from CN.
C2F = sl next 2 sts onto CN and
leave at front of work, K2, then
K2 from CN.

CABLE PATTERN

Worked over 34 sts.
1st row (rs facing) P1, *K2, P2,
K4, P2, rep from * to last 3 sts,
K2, P1.
2nd row K1, P2, *K2, P4, K2,
P2, rep from * to last st, K1.
3rd row P1, K2, P2, K4, P2, K2,
P2, C2F, P2, K2, P2, K4, P2, K2,
P1.
4th row As 2nd row.
Rep 1st and 2nd rows once more.

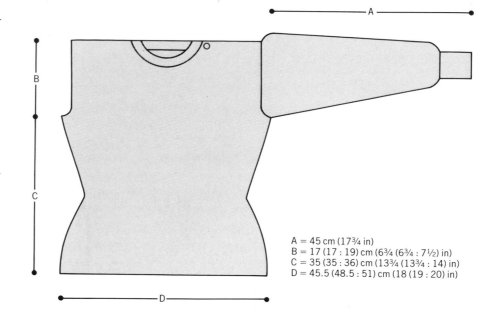

A = 45 cm (17¾ in)
B = 17 (17 : 19) cm (6¾ (6¾ : 7½) in)
C = 35 (35 : 36) cm (13¾ (13¾ : 14) in)
D = 45.5 (48.5 : 51) cm (18 (19 : 20) in)

7th row P1, Cr3B, Cr3F, P2,
C2B, P2, Cr3B, Cr3F, P1.
8th row As 2nd row.
These 8 rows form the *cable pattern*
and are rep as required.

BACK

With 2mm (US 00) needles cast
on 145(153:161) sts.
1st row K tbl.
2nd row K.
3rd row P.
Change to 3mm (US 2) needles
and work in patt as foll:
1st row (rs facing) (P1, K1)
13(15:17) times, now work across
1st row of *cable pattern* over next 34
sts, K1, (P1, K1) 12 times, now

work across 1st row of *cable pattern*
over next 34 sts, (K1, P1)
13(15:17) times.
2nd row (P1, K1) 13(15:17)
times, work across 2nd row of *cable
pattern*, K1, (P1, K1) 12 times,
work across 2nd row of *cable
pattern*, (K1, P1) 13(15:17) times.
Cont as now set, working each
side of cable patt in moss st, and
working cable patt until 8 patt
rows have been worked.
Dec row (rs facing) Moss st
11(13:15) sts, sl 1, K2 tog, psso,
moss st 12(14:16) sts, work across
1st row of *cable pattern* over next 34
sts, moss st 11 sts, sl 1, K2 tog,
psso, moss st 11 sts, work across
1st row of *cable pattern* over next 34
sts, moss st 12(14:16) sts, sl 1, K2
tog, psso, moss st 11(13:15) sts.
(139(147:155) sts)
Cont in patt as set, *at the same time,*
work a dec row on every foll 6th
row working decs directly above
previous decs. (6 sts are dec on
each dec row.)
Cont as set until 103(111:119) sts
rem, and 7 dec rows have been
worked.
Cont straight in patt as set until
back measures 17cm (6¾in) from
cast-on edge, ending with a ws
row.

Inc row Moss st 2 sts, M1, moss st 10(14:18) sts, M1, work *cable pattern* over next 34 sts, M1, moss st 11 sts, M1, work *cable pattern* over next 24 sts, M1, moss st 10(14:18) sts, M1, moss st 2 sts. (109(117:125) sts)

Cont in patt as set, *at the same time*, work an inc row on every foll 8th row working incs in positions as set. (6 sts are inc on each inc row.)

Cont as set until there are 145(153:161) sts on the needle, and 7 inc rows have been worked.

Now cont straight in patt until back measures 35(35:36)cm (13¾(13¾:14¼)in) from cast-on edge, ending with a ws row.

Shape armholes

Keeping patt correct, cast off 5 sts at beg of next 2 rows.

Now dec 1 st at both ends of next row and every foll alt row until 103(107:111) sts rem.

Now cont straight until back measures 52(52:55)cm (20½(20½:21¾)in) from cast-on edge, ending with a ws row.

Cast off all sts loosely.

FRONT

Work as for back until front measures 45(45:47)cm (17¾(17¾:18½)in) from cast-on edge, ending with a ws row. (103(107:111) sts)

Shape front neck

Next row Patt 39(41:43), cast off centre 25 sts, patt to end of row and cont on last set of 39(41:43) sts only.

**Keeping patt correct, dec 1 st at neck edge on every row until 28(30:32) sts rem.

Now work straight until front measures same as back to cast-off shoulder edge, ending with a ws row.

Cast off loosely.

With ws facing rejoin yarn to rem sts and work as for first side from ** to end.

SLEEVES

With 2mm (US 00) needles cast on 56(56:60) sts and work in K2, P2, rib for 7cm (2¾in).

Inc row P and inc 8(8:4) sts evenly across row. (64 sts)

Change to 3mm (US 2) needles and work in patt as foll:

1st row (rs facing) Moss st 15 sts, work across 1st row of *cable pattern* over next 34 sts, moss st 15 sts.

Cont in patt as now set until sleeve measures 12cm (4¾in) from cast-on edge, ending with a ws row.

Inc row Moss st 2 sts, M1, moss st 13 sts, M1, *cable pattern* over next 34 sts, M1, moss st 13 sts, M1, moss st 2 sts. (68 sts)

Cont in patt as set, *at the same time*, work an inc row on every foll 8th row in positions as set until there are 112 sts on the needle, and 12 inc rows have been worked. (4 sts are inc on each inc row.)

Now cont straight until sleeve measures 45cm (17¾in) from cast-on edge, ending with a ws row.

Shape top

Keeping patt correct, cast off 5 sts at beg of next 2 rows.

Now dec 1 st at both ends of next row and every foll alt row until 54(54:36) sts rem.

Now dec 1 st at both ends of every row until 24 sts rem.

Cast off.

Rep patt for second sleeve.

NECKBAND

Join right shoulder seam carefully matching patt.

With 2mm (US 00) needles and rs facing, pick up and K 29 sts down left front neck, 25 sts across centre front, 29 sts up right front neck and finally 49 sts across back neck. (132 sts)

Next row (ws facing) Cast on 4 sts, work in K2, P2, rib to end of row. (136 sts)

Cont in double rib as set for 2 rows.

Buttonhole row (rs facing) Rib 4, yrn, K2 tog, rib to end.

Work a further 4 rows in rib.

Cast off fairly loosely ribwise.

SHOULDER PADS

With 2mm (US 00) needles cast on 41 sts.

1st row K1, *P1, K1, rep from * to end.

2nd row P1, *K1, P1, rep from * to end.

Keeping rib as now set, dec 1 st at both ends of every row until 3 sts rem.

Next row Sl 1, K2 tog, psso.

Pull yarn through rem st and secure.

Rep patt for second shoulder pad.

TO MAKE UP

Join left shoulder seam, *do not* join side edges of neckband. Join side and sleeve seams. Set sleeves into armholes, gathering fullness evenly across top of shoulder. Sew shoulder pads in place. (See note on shoulder pads on page 11.)

Sew button on neckband to correspond with buttonhole.

CABBAGE ROSE SWEATER

I wanted to put oversized roses on a huge, floppy sweater, and the result is very strong. It turned out to be one of our most successful designs ever and the press in particular liked it a lot, turning it into a kind of Edina Ronay trademark. Almost all my friends seem to have one, especially the version we made with cream roses on black. You could also make it with bright colours on a yellow or black background.

MEASUREMENTS

One size only to fit bust
91–107cm (36–42in).
Actual measurement
132cm (52in).
Full length 75cm (29½in).
Sleeve seam 46cm (18in).

MATERIALS

Rowan Handknit D.K. Cotton
50g balls.
Main colour (MC) ecru (251)
18 balls;
1st contrast colour (A) cherry
(298) 2 balls;
2nd contrast colour (B) clover
(266) 2 balls;
3rd contrast colour (C) black
(252) 1 ball;
4th contrast colour (D) yellow
(271) 1 ball.
Equivalent yarn: D.K.
1 pair each of 4mm (US 5) and
4½mm (US 6) knitting needles.
2 spare needles.

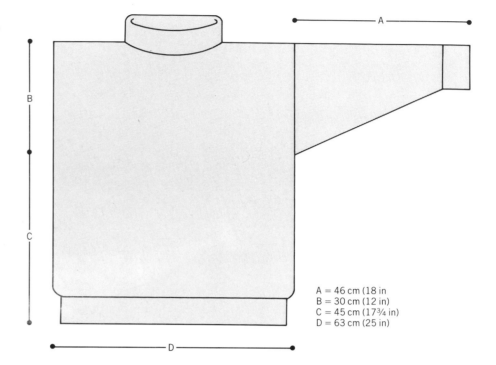

A = 46 cm (18 in)
B = 30 cm (12 in)
C = 45 cm (17¾ in)
D = 63 cm (25 in)

TENSION

18 sts and 24 rows to 10cm (4in)
on 4½mm (US 6) needles over
st st. See page 10.

BACK

With 4mm (US 5) needles and
MC, cast on 120 sts and work in
K2, P2, rib for 7cm (2¾in).
Change to 4½mm (US 6) needles
and starting with a K row work 20
rows in st st.

Place first chart

1st row (rs facing) K24MC, now
K across the 40 sts of 1st row of
chart, K56MC.

2nd row P56MC, P across the 40
sts of 2nd row of chart, P24MC.
The chart is now placed. Cont as
set until 50 rows of chart are
worked.

Place second chart

Next row (rs facing) K24MC, K
across the 40 sts of 51st row of
chart, K4MC, now K across the
40 sts of 1st row of chart, K12MC.

Next row P12MC, P across the
40 sts of 2nd row of chart, P4MC,
now P across the 40 sts of 52nd
row of chart, P24MC.
Cont working both charts as now
placed until first motif is
complete.
Cont to work 2nd motif until 54
rows of chart have been worked.

Place third chart

Next row (rs facing) K8MC, K

across the 40 sts of 1st row of chart, K20MC, K across the 40 sts of 55th row of chart, K12MC.
Next row P12MC, P across the 40 sts of 56th row of chart, P20MC, P across the 40 sts of 2nd row of chart, P8MC.
Cont working both charts as now placed until 2nd motif is complete.
Cont to work 3rd motif until the 60 rows of chart are complete, thus ending with a ws row.
Now starting with a K row work 4 rows in st st in MC.
Next row Cast off 37 sts, leave next 46 sts on a spare needle, cast off rem 37 sts.

FRONT
Work as for back until 50 rows of third motif have been worked.

Shape front neck
Next row (rs facing) Patt 47, leave next 26 sts on a spare needle, K rem sts and work on this last set of 47 sts only.
**Dec 1 st at neck edge on next 10 rows. (37 sts)
Now work a few rows straight until front measures same as back to cast-off shoulder edge, ending with a ws row.
Cast off.
With ws facing rejoin yarn to rem sts, and keeping patt correct, work as for first side from ** to end.

RIGHT SLEEVE
With 4mm (US 5) needles and MC, cast on 44 sts and work in K2, P2, rib for 7cm (2¾in).
Inc row Rib and inc 8 sts evenly across row. (52 sts)

Change to 4½mm (US 6) needles and starting with a K row work 12 rows in st st, *at the same time*, inc 1 st at both ends of 6th row and then foll 3rd rows twice. (58 sts)
Place chart
1st row (rs facing) K9MC, now K across the 40 sts of 1st row of chart, K9MC.
Next row P9MC, P across the 40 sts of 2nd row of chart, P9MC.
Cont to foll chart as now placed, *at the same time*, inc 1 st at both ends of next row and then every foll 3rd row until there are 108 sts on the needle, and when chart is complete cont in MC only.
Now work a few rows straight until sleeve measures 46cm (18in) from cast-on edge, ending with a ws row.
Cast off fairly loosely.

LEFT SLEEVE
Work as for right sleeve but work throughout in MC, omitting all reference to chart.

ROLL COLLAR
Join right shoulder seam.
With 4mm (US 5) needles and rs facing and MC, pick up and K8 sts down left front neck, then K across 26 sts at centre front, inc 8 sts evenly across, then pick up and K8 sts up right front neck, and then K across the 46 sts at back neck, inc 16 sts evenly across. (112 sts)
Work in K2, P2, rib for 30cm (12in).
Cast off fairly loosely ribwise.

TO MAKE UP
Join left shoulder seam and roll collar, reversing seam for turn back. With centre of cast-off edges of sleeves to shoulder seams, sew sleeves carefully in position reaching down to same depth on front and back. Join side and sleeve seams. Roll collar onto right side.

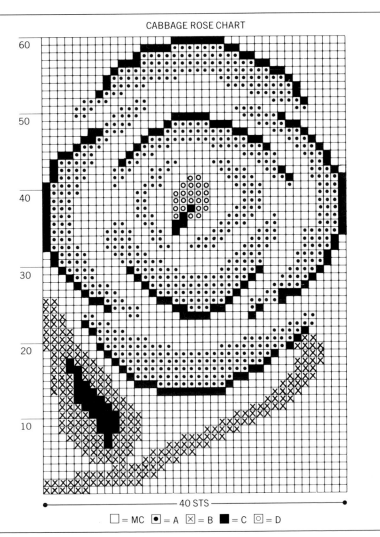

CABBAGE ROSE CHART

40 STS

□ = MC ● = A ⊠ = B ■ = C ⊙ = D

PASTEL
FAIR ISLES

This summertime Fair Isle can be made up for men or women. The ladies' sweater has a gentle, slightly gathered sleeve, making it feminine and flattering to wear. The men's sweater has more of a square shape and a drop shoulder. The muted natural tones I have used in the photograph are classic Fair Isle colours, popular all over the world.

PASTEL
FAIR ISLE
FOR WOMEN

MEASUREMENTS

To fit bust 86(91:97)cm
(34(36:38)in).
Actual measurement
91(96:100)cm (36(37¾:39½)in).
Full length 55(56:56)cm
(21¾(22:22)in).
Sleeve seam approx 45cm
(17¾in).

MATERIALS

Rowan Cabled Mercerised Cotton
50g balls.
Main colour (MC) cream (301)
8(8:9) balls;
1st contrast colour (A) navy (330)
2(2:2) balls;
2nd contrast colour (B) granit
(325) 2(2:2) balls;
3rd contrast colour (C) thyme
(329) 1(1:1) ball;
4th contrast colour (D) terracotta
(314) 1(1:1) ball;
5th contrast colour (E) olive (327)
1(1:1) ball.
Equivalent yarn: 3-ply.
1 pair each of 2¼mm (US 0) and
3mm (US 2) knitting needles.
2 spare needles.

TENSION

34 sts and 36 rows to 10cm (4in)
on 3mm (US 2) needles over Fair
Isle patt. See page 10.

BACK

With 2¼mm (US 0) needles and
MC, cast on 126(132:138) sts and
work in K1, P1, rib for 10cm
(4in).
Inc row Rib and inc 29(31:33) sts
evenly across row. (155(163:171)
sts)
Change to 3mm (US 2) needles
and starting with a K row work in
st st from chart as foll:
1st row (rs facing) Work 1 st
before the dotted line, rep the 8 st

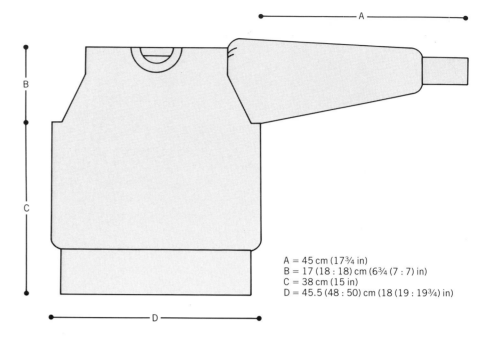

A = 45 cm (17¾ in)
B = 17 (18 : 18) cm (6¾ (7 : 7) in)
C = 38 cm (15 in)
D = 45.5 (48 : 50) cm (18 (19 : 19¾) in)

patt to last 2 sts, work 2 sts
beyond the dotted line.
2nd row Work 2 sts before the
dotted line, rep the 8 st patt to last
st, work 1 st beyond the dotted
line.
Cont in patt as set until the 44
rows of chart are worked.
Now work rows 17–28.
Cont to rep these 56 rows in
sequence as set until back
measures 38cm (15in) from
cast-on edge, ending with a ws
row.
Shape armholes
Cast off 5 sts at beg of next 2 rows.
Keeping patt correct, cast off 2 sts
at beg of next 6 rows.
Now dec 1 st at both ends of every
foll alt row until 107(113:119) sts
rem.
Now cont straight until back
measures 55(56:56)cm
(21¾(22:22)in) from cast-on
edge, ending with a ws row.
Shape shoulders
Cast off 30(32:34) sts at beg of
next 2 rows.
Leave rem 47(49:51) sts on a
spare needle.

FRONT

Work as for back until front

measures 49(50:50)cm
(19¼(19¾:19¾)in) from cast-on
edge, ending with a ws row
(armhole shaping is complete).
Shape front neck
Next row Patt 39(42:45), turn,
work 2 tog, patt to end of row
and cont on this last set of

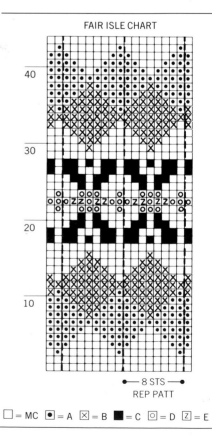

FAIR ISLE CHART

40

30

20

10

●—— 8 STS ——●
REP PATT

□ = MC ●• = A ⊠ = B ■ = C ⊙ = D ☑ = E

38(41:44) sts only.
**Keeping patt correct, dec 1 st at neck edge on every row until 30(32:34) sts rem.
Now cont straight until front measures same as back to cast-off shoulder edge, ending at side edge.
Cast off.
Return to rem sts and sl centre 29 sts onto a spare needle, with rs facing rejoin yarn to rem sts and patt to end of row.

Next row Patt to last 2 sts, work 2 tog.
Now work as for first side from ** to end.

SLEEVES
With 2¼mm (US 0) needles and MC, cast on 66(68:70) sts and work in K1, P1, rib for 10cm (4in).
Inc row Rib and inc 41(39:37) sts evenly across row. (107 sts)
Change to 3mm (US 2) needles and starting with a K row work in st st from chart, starting on 29th row as foll:
29th row (rs facing) Work 1 st before the dotted line, rep the 8 st patt to last 2 sts, work 2 sts beyond the dotted line.
Cont in patt as set, working patt rows as for back, *at the same time* inc 1 st at both ends of every foll 20th row until there are 111 sts on the needle, working inc sts into patt.
Now cont straight until sleeve measures approx 45cm (17¾in) from cast-on edge, ending on a ws row, and same patt row as back/front to beg of armhole shaping.
Shape top
Cast off 5 sts at beg of next 2 rows.
Keeping patt correct, cast off 2 sts at beg of next 6 rows.
Now dec 1 st at *beg only* of next 20(20:16) rows. (69(69:73) sts)
Work 20(22:26) rows straight.
Dec 1 st at beg of next 6 rows.
Cast off 2 sts at beg of next 4 rows.
Cast off 3 sts at beg of foll 4 rows.
Next row K1, (K2 tog) across row.
Cast off fairly loosely.
Rep patt for second sleeve.

NECKBAND
Join right shoulder seam.
With 2¼mm (US 0) needles and MC and rs facing, pick up and K 32 sts down left front neck, K across centre front sts, pick up and K 32 sts up right front neck, and finally K across back neck sts. (140(142:144) sts)
Work in K1, P1, rib for 7 rows.
Cast off fairly loosely ribwise.

TO MAKE UP
Join left shoulder and neckband seam. Join side and sleeve seams matching patts. Set sleeves carefully into armholes, gathering fullness evenly across top of shoulder.

PASTEL
FAIR ISLE
FOR MEN

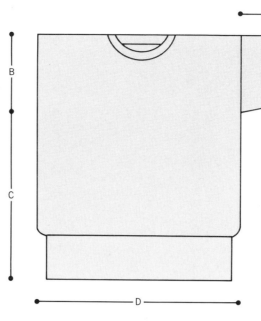

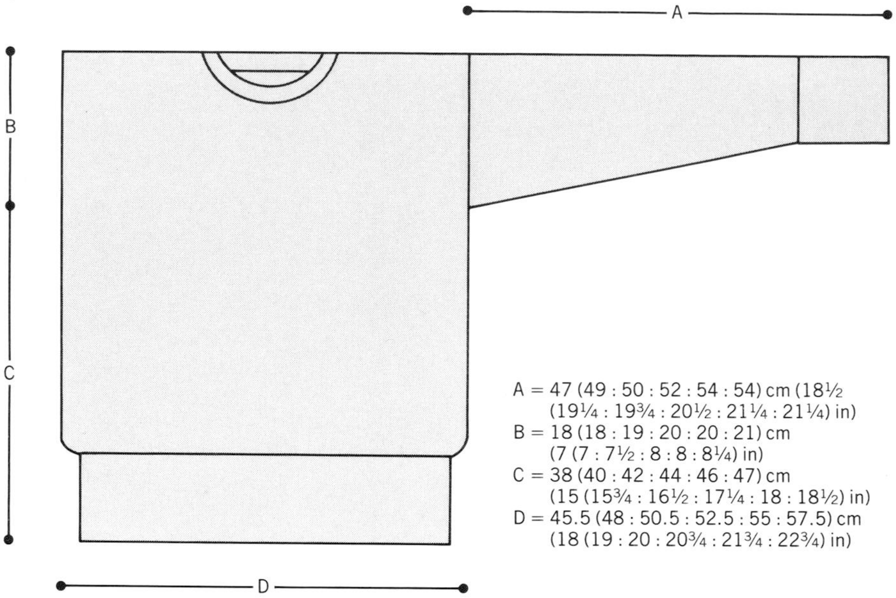

A = 47 (49 : 50 : 52 : 54 : 54) cm (18½
  (19¼ : 19¾ : 20½ : 21¼ : 21¼) in)
B = 18 (18 : 19 : 20 : 20 : 21) cm
  (7 (7 : 7½ : 8 : 8 : 8¼) in)
C = 38 (40 : 42 : 44 : 46 : 47) cm
  (15 (15¾ : 16½ : 17¼ : 18 : 18½) in)
D = 45.5 (48 : 50.5 : 52.5 : 55 : 57.5) cm
  (18 (19 : 20 : 20¾ : 21¾ : 22¾) in)

MEASUREMENTS

To fit chest
86(91:97:102:107:112)cm
(34(36:38:40:42:44)in).
Actual measurement
91(96:101:105:110:115)cm
(36(37¾:39¾:41½:43¼:45¼)in).
Full length 56(58:61:64:66:68)cm
(22(22¾:24:25¼:26:26¾)in).
Sleeve seam 47(49:50:52:54:54)cm
(18½(19¼:19¾:20½:21¼:21¼)in)

MATERIALS

Rowan Cabled Mercerised Cotton
50g balls.
Main colour (MC) cream (301)
9(9:10:10:11:11) balls;
1st contrast colour (A) black
(319) 3(3:3:3:4:4) balls;
2nd contrast colour (B) granit
(325) 3(3:3:3:4:4) balls;
3rd contrast colour (C) souris
(318) 2(2:2:2:3:3) balls;
4th contrast colour (D) thyme
(329) 2(2:2:2:3:3) balls;

5th contrast colour (E) olive (327)
1(1:1:1:2:2) ball(s).
Equivalent yarn: 3-ply.
1 pair each of 2¼mm (US 0) and
3mm (US 2) knitting needles.
2 spare needles.

TENSION

34 sts and 36 rows to 10cm (4in)
on 3mm (US 2) needles over Fair
Isle patt. See page 10.

CHART NOTE

The Fair Isle chart for this patt is
the same as the chart for the
Pastel Fair Isle for Women (see
page 150).

BACK

With 2¼mm (US 0) needles and
MC, cast on 140(144:150:160:
166:172) sts and work in K1, P1,
rib for 10cm (4in).
Inc row Rib and inc
15(19:21:19:21:23) sts evenly
across row.
(155(163:171:179:187:195) sts)
Change to 3mm (US 2) needles
and starting with a K row work in
st st from chart as foll:
1st row (rs facing) Work 1 st
before the dotted line, rep the 8 st
patt to last 2 sts, work 2 sts
beyond the dotted line.
2nd row Work 2 sts before the
dotted line, rep the 8 st patt to last
st, work 1 st beyond the dotted
line.
Cont in patt as set until the 44
rows of chart are worked.
Now work rows 17–28.
Cont to rep these 56 rows in
sequence as set until back
measures 56(58:61:64:66:68)cm
(22(22¾:24:25¼:26:26¾)in)
from cast-on edge, ending with

a ws row.
Shape shoulders
Cast off 52(55:58:61:63:67) sts at
beg of next 2 rows.
Leave rem 51(53:55:57:61:61) sts
on a spare needle.

FRONT

Work as for back until front
measures 48(50:53:56:58:60)cm
(19(19¾:21:22:22¾:23½)in) from
cast-on edge, ending with a ws
row.
Shape front neck
Next row Patt 64(68:72:76:
78:82), turn, work 2 tog, patt to
end of row and cont on this last set
of 63(67:71:75:77:81) sts only.
**Keeping patt correct, dec 1 st
at neck edge on every row until
52(55:58:61:63:67) sts rem.
Now cont straight until front
measures same as back to cast-off
shoulder edge, ending at side
edge. Cast off.
Return to rem sts and slip centre
27(27:27:27:31:31) sts onto a
spare needle, with rs facing rejoin
yarn to rem sts and patt to end of
row.
Next row Patt to last 2 sts, work
2 tog.
Now work as for first side from **
to end.

SLEEVES

With 2¼mm (US 0) needles and
MC, cast on 66(66:66:74:74:74)
sts and work in K1, P1, rib for
10cm (4in), inc 1 st on last row
only. (67(67:67:75:75:75) sts)
Change to 3mm (US 2) needles
and starting with a K row work in
st st from chart, placing chart as
for back and working patt rows as
for back, *at the same time*, inc 1 st at
both ends of every foll 4th row
until there are 127(133:135:141:
145:145) sts on the needle,
working inc sts into patt.
Now cont straight until sleeve
measures 47(49:50:52:54:54)cm
(18½(19¼:19¾:20½:21¼:21¼)in)

from cast-on edge, ending with a
ws row.
Cast off fairly loosely.
Rep patt for second sleeve.

NECKBAND

Join right shoulder seam.
With 2¼mm (US 0) needles and
MC and rs facing, pick up and K
34 sts down left front neck, K
across centre front sts, pick up
and K 34 sts up right front neck
and finally K across centre back

sts. (146(148:150:152:160:160)
sts)
Work in K1, P1, rib for 7 rows.
Cast off fairly loosely ribwise.

TO MAKE UP

Join left shoulder and neckband
seam. With centre of cast-off
edges of sleeves to shoulder seams,
sew sleeves carefully in position
reaching down to same patt row
on front and back. Join side and
sleeve seams matching patt.

TYROLEAN CARDIGAN

The pattern on this cardigan, which continues around the back as well, was inspired by a piece of old lace in one of my books. I think the colours, the silver buttons and the edelweiss-type flowers give it a Tyrolean look. In my collection, I matched it with some brightly coloured peasant skirts covered in silver and pewter beads. If you want to try a different effect, the pattern looks equally good on a black background.

MEASUREMENTS

To fit bust 86–97(102–107)cm
(34–38(40–42)in).
Actual measurement 107(116)cm
(42(45¾)in).
Full length 43(45)cm
(17(17¾)in).
Sleeve seam 43cm (17in).

MATERIALS

Rowan Handknit D.K. Cotton
50g balls.
Main colour (MC) ecru (251)
13(14) balls;
1st contrast colour (A) clover
(266) 1(1) ball.
Rowan Fine Cotton Chenille
50g balls (used double).
2nd contrast colour (B) cardinal
(379) 2(2) balls;
3rd contrast colour (C) cyclamen
(385) 1(1) ball.
Equivalent yarn: D.K. used
throughout.
1 pair each of 3¾mm (US 4) and
4mm (US 5) knitting needles.
8 buttons.
Spare needle.

TENSION

20 sts and 28 rows to 10cm (4in)
on 4mm (US 5) needles over st st
using MC. See page 10.

BACK

With 3¾mm (US 4) needles and

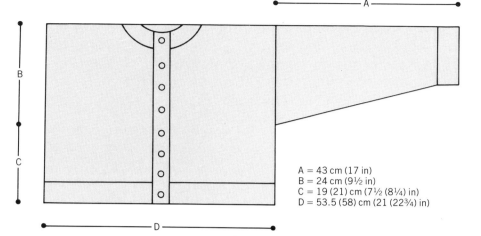

A = 43 cm (17 in)
B = 24 cm (9½ in)
C = 19 (21) cm (7½ (8¼) in)
D = 53.5 (58) cm (21 (22¾) in)

MC, cast on 104(112) sts and
work in K2, P2, rib for 5cm
(2in).
Inc row Rib and inc 3 sts evenly
across row. (107(115) sts)
Change to 4mm (US 5) needles
and starting with a K row work in
st st working from *back chart*,
working between appropriate
lines for size required.
When 23 rows of chart have been
worked, cont straight in MC only
until 101(105) rows have been
worked from top of rib, thus
ending with a rs row.
Shape back neck
Next row P40(44) sts, turn, work
2 tog and K to end of row and
work on this last set of 39(43) sts
only.
**Dec 1 st at neck edge on every

row until 36(40) sts rem. (106(110)
rows worked from top of rib.)
Cast off.
Return to rem sts and sl centre 27
sts on to a spare needle, with ws
facing rejoin yarn to rem sts and P
to end of row.
Next row K to last 2 sts, work 2
tog.
Now work as for first side from **
to end.

RIGHT FRONT

With 3¾mm (US 4) needles and
MC, cast on 48(52) sts and work
in K2, P2, rib for 5cm (2in).
Inc row Rib and inc 2(3) sts
evenly across row. (50(55) sts)
Change to 4mm (US 5) needles
and starting with a K row work in
st st from *right front chart*, working

BACK CHART

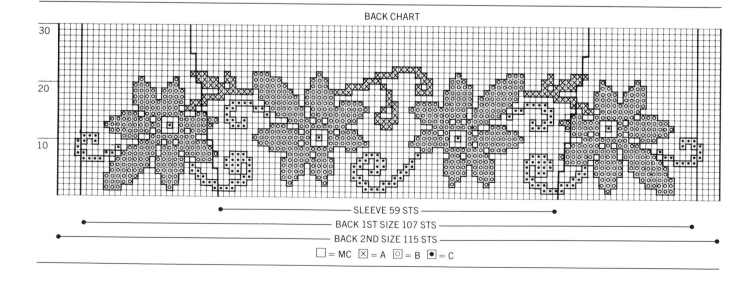

SLEEVE 59 STS
BACK 1ST SIZE 107 STS
BACK 2ND SIZE 115 STS

□ = MC ☒ = A ⊙ = B ▣ = C

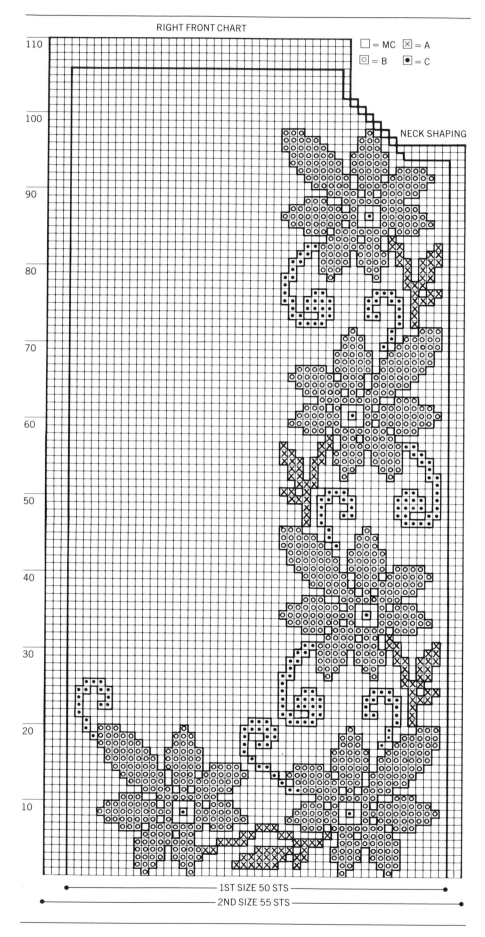

RIGHT FRONT CHART

□ = MC ⊠ = A
⊙ = B ⦿ = C

NECK SHAPING

110
100
90
80
70
60
50
40
30
20
10

1ST SIZE 50 STS
2ND SIZE 55 STS

between appropriate lines for size required.

Cont foll chart until 94(96) rows have been worked, thus ending with a ws row.

Shape front neck
Cast off 6(9) sts at beg of next row.
Keeping chart correct, dec 1 st at neck edge on every row until 36(40) sts rem. Now cont straight until the 106(110) rows of chart have been worked. Cast off.

LEFT FRONT

With 3¾mm (US 4) needles and MC, cast on 48(52) sts and work in K2, P2, rib for 5cm (2in).
Inc row Rib and inc 2(3) sts evenly across row. (50(55) sts)
Change to 4mm (US 5) needles.
Now starting with a P row (ws row), work in st st from *right front chart* (this reverses chart and front).
Complete as for right front, working odd numbered rows as P rows (reading from right to left) and even numbered rows as K rows (reading from left to right).

SLEEVES

With 3¾mm (US 4) needles and MC cast on 48 sts and work in K2, P2, rib for 5cm (2in).
Inc row Rib and inc 11 sts evenly across row. (59 sts)
Change to 4mm (US 5) needles and starting with a K row work in st st from *back chart* (foll *sleeve shaping lines* as indicated). When 23 rows of chart have been worked cont in MC only, and inc 1 st at both ends of every foll 5th row as set until there are 99 sts on the needle.
Now cont straight until sleeve measures 43cm (17in) from cast-on edge, ending with a ws row.
Cast off fairly loosely.
Rep patt for second sleeve.

BUTTONHOLE BAND

With 3¾mm (US 4) needles and MC and rs facing, pick up and K 104 sts evenly up right front edge.

Work in K2, P2, rib for 2cm (¾in).

Buttonhole row (rs facing) Rib 3, cast off 2 sts, *rib 14, cast off 2 sts, rep from * to last 3 sts, rib 3.

Next row Rib, casting on 2 sts over cast-off sts on previous row. (7 buttonholes worked.)

Now cont in rib until band measures 4cm (1½in).

Cast off fairly loosely ribwise.

BUTTON BAND

Work as for buttonhole band, but omitting buttonholes.

NECKBAND

Join both shoulder seams.

With 3¾mm (US 4) needles and MC and rs facing, pick up and K 26 across buttonhole band and up right front neck, K across back neck sts, inc 9 sts evenly across, and finally pick up and K 26 sts down left front neck and button band. (88 sts)

Work in K2, P2, rib for 2cm (¾in).

Buttonhole row (rs facing) Rib 4, cast off 2 sts, rib to end.

Next row Rib, casting on 2 sts over cast-off sts on previous row. Now cont in rib until neckband measures 4cm (1½in).

Cast off fairly loosely ribwise.

TO MAKE UP

With centre of cast-off edges of sleeves to shoulder seams, sew sleeves carefully in position reaching down to same depth on front and back. Join side and sleeve seams. Sew on buttons to correspond with buttonholes.

YARN SUPPLIERS

Although the yarns used for the sweaters in this book are from the Rowan Yarns range, all patterns can be knitted using 'equivalent yarn' from other spinners as mentioned at the foot of each 'Materials' section, however in such cases the quantities needed may vary.
For details of Rowan Yarns stockists please contact:

AUSTRALIA

Sunspun Enterprises Pty Ltd
195 Canterbury Road
Canterbury
3126 Victoria
Telephone 03 830 1609

BERMUDA

The Yarn Loft
PO Box DV 203
Devonshire
DV BX
Telephone 809 29 5 0551

CANADA

Estelle Designs & Sales Ltd
38 Continental Place
Scarborough
Ontario
M1R 2T4
Telephone 416 298 9922

CYPRUS

Litsa Christofides
Colourworks
12 Parnithos Street
Nicosia
Telephone 357 472933

DENMARK

Mosekonens Vaerksted
Mosevej 13
Li Binderup
9600 Aars
Telephone 45 8 656065

HOLLAND

Henk and Henrietta Beukers
Dorpstraat 9
5327 AR Hurwenen
Telephone 31 4182 1764

ITALY

Daniela Basso & Co
La Campagnia del Cotone
Corso Matteotti, 35
10121 Torino
Telephone 011 878381

JAPAN

Diakeito Co Ltd
1-5-23 Nakatsu
Oyodo-Ku
Osaka 531
Telephone 06 371 5653

NEW ZEALAND

Creative Fashion Centre
PO Box 45083
Epuni Railway
Lower Hutt
Telephone 04 664 689

NORWAY

Jorun Sandin
Eureka
Kvakkestandgarden
1400 Ski
Telephone 0287 1909

SWEDEN

Eva Wincent Gelinder
Wincent
Luntmakargatan, 56
113 58 Stockholm
Telephone 08 32 70 60

UNITED KINGDOM

Rowan Yarns
Green Lane Mill
Holmfirth
West Yorkshire
HD7 1RW
Telephone 0484 681881

UNITED STATES

Westminster Trading
Corporation
5 Northern Boulevard
Amherst
New Hampshire 03031
Telephone 603 886 5041

WEST GERMANY

Beatrijs Sterk
Friedenstrasse, 5
3000 Hanover 1
Telephone 0511 818001